The Angler's Mail guide to

Basic Coarse Fishing

The Angler's Mail guide to

Basic
Coarse Fishing

Consultant editors: John Ingham & Roy Westwood

Hamlyn
London · New York · Sydney · Toronto

Contributors

John Bailey
Andy Barker
John Essex
Jim Gibbinson
Dave Litton
Graham Marsden
Peter Mohan
John Neville
Peter Stone
John Weedon
John Wilson

Title spread An angler
trotting the stream for
chub.

This page Match fishing
on a lowland river.

Contents and back jacket
Returning three 8 lb bream
and a 4 lb 4 oz roach
X bream hybrid to the
water.

Published by The Hamlyn Publishing Group Limited
London · New York · Sydney · Toronto
Astronaut House, Feltham, Middlesex, England.

Copyright © The Hamlyn Publishing Group Limited 1981
ISBN 0 600 35386 9

Second Impression 1981

Phototypeset by Photocomp Ltd. Birmingham, England
Printed in Spain by Graficromo, S.A. Córdoba

Contents

Introduction

The beginner who as a boy learns to fish with his father gets a perfect baptism in the sport. His father takes him fishing, introduces him to various types of water, the different species of fish and a wide range of angling methods and baits. But what of the newcomer who does not have this advantage? And not all beginners are youngsters — many adults take up fishing, sometimes quite late in life. How do such newcomers find their way through what appears to be a complicated maze of regulations and restrictions — and how do they find somewhere to go fishing when almost every lake or stretch of river seems to be guarded by 'Private' or 'No Fishing' signs?

The first requirement is a Water Authority rod licence for your area. You cannot legally fish in any lake, pond, pit, river, canal or stream until you have the appropriate rod licence. These can be bought from your local fishing tackle shop, and most authorities have special concessionary rates for juniors or pensioners. Make sure that you buy an annual licence or one that will cover you for the whole of the fishing season. Do not make the mistake of buying a short-term licence, because these are only economic if you are in an area for a short while, and do not intend to fish the water regularly.

Fishing waters fall into one of four main categories:

1. **Private** — those on which fishing is not allowed at all, or where rights are strictly controlled.
2. **Club** — where the rights are owned or controlled by an angling club which is open to members on payment of an annual subscription. Fees vary but usually fall in the £2 to £12 per year range. Reduced rates are sometimes available for youngsters or pensioners. Some clubs are very easy to join — you simply send the club secretary your subscription, and perhaps an entrance fee, and you are in. Others have waiting-lists.
3. **Day Ticket** — these might be privately owned, leased by a club or owned by the local council (many public park lakes, for example, are council-controlled). Such waters can be fished by anyone who purchases the necessary day-ticket. Sometimes the ticket needs to be obtained in advance — possibly from a local tackle shop, but usually a water bailiff collects the ticket money while you are fishing. Average day-ticket prices are in the 50p to £1 range.
4. **Free** — few waters offer completely free access. Fishing rights are almost always held by someone, but sometimes the owner does not exercise his ownership and anglers fish free of charge. These may be farm ponds that can be fished with the farmer's permission, flooded quarry pits or brick pits and relatively small streams.

How do you discover the whereabouts of fishing waters in your area? First ask at your local tackle shop — if the owner is a knowledgeable angler this might give you some really valuable information. He should certainly provide membership particulars about local clubs. Then a good idea is to get hold of an Ordnance Survey map and actually visit all the likely-looking lakes, ponds and rivers within reasonable travelling distance of your home. Weekends are a good time for these exploratory visits because if there are fish in the water you will very likely find someone fishing. A polite enquiry will invariably reveal who owns the water, what fish are in it and all the other information you are likely to need. Sometimes the conversation leads to information about other waters. If you intend fishing regularly it is apparent that the best bet is to join a club. Not only is it the cheapest way of getting access to waters, but club fisheries generally offer better quality sport than day-ticket waters. Another advantage of club membership is that many of them run all sorts of activities that are of great benefit to a newcomer:

Opposite An angler lake fishing with all his tackle and accessories close to hand.

13

One of the hazards of fishing from the water itself is the attention of inquisitive birds like this pair of swans!

films, talks, instructional evenings and competitions. As well as learning about fishing you will meet other anglers.

Assuming that you have bought your licence and joined a local angling club, you are now ready to go fishing. Tomorrow morning you intend getting up early, filling your flask and heading for your chosen water. Well, maybe . . . but there are a few more things you need to know.

You may not fish for coarse fish in England between March 15 and June 15 — that period is known as the Close Season and exists to permit the fish to breed uninterrupted.

On some waters there might be special regulations — one of the most common restricts fishing to the period between dawn and dusk. Sometimes you will encounter a limit on the number of rods you may use, or a ban on the use of certain baits.

It is very likely that you will have already decided where you are going for your first fishing trip. The chances are that it will be somewhere that has been recommended to you, or perhaps where you watched somebody catching some good fish. However, if you have not yet made up your mind, a pond is a good starting point — preferably quite a small pond. There are more than 330,000 in England and Wales, mostly in the south. Some are natural, some have been created by digging holes or damming streams. In bygone times they were used to provide drinking water for farm livestock or village horses and as an extra food source many were stocked with fish. Most small ponds hold roach; many will hold rudd. Bream and tench may be found in some of them and in the south crucian carp are probable. The common factor is that the fish are likely to be small, plentiful and easy to catch. At one time most ponds held perch, but sadly this species has been decimated by disease and is only just showing signs of recovery. Perch are the ideal beginner's fish, being very free biting at all times of the year and in all weather.

Although ponds are likely to hold teeming hoards of small fish, that is not always the case. Some ponds hold big carp, tench or even pike. If the pond is in any way connected to a river, such as via a ditch or small stream, it will probably hold eels. These, too, could be big.

This is the marvellous thing about fishing — you never know what a water may hold. Everyone may tell you that a certain water is full of, say, stunted rudd, that there is nothing in there bigger than 4-5 oz, then right out of the blue someone catches a two-pounder — which is a very big rudd — or perhaps a 4 lb tench or double-figure carp. You will soon learn that not all days are equally good. Generally fish are difficult to catch if the sun is bright and there is no breeze to ruffle the water. If, on the

Canals like this one which is partially weeded can often provide the angler with an enjoyable day's sport.

other hand, the day is overcast and there is a gentle breeze, then fish may feed well. Non-anglers seem to think that fishermen love rain because that is when fish supposedly bite best, but in practice heavy rain is frequently detrimental. Prolonged rain also has a long-term effect. It results in rivers, streams and stream-fed stillwaters becoming high and coloured. In extreme conditions flooding may occur. A hard overnight frost can also make things difficult.

Generally in summer and autumn fish feed best in the early morning. In winter the evening is often the best time. Usually fish are easiest to catch when it is warm. Winter fishing can be hard — if the weather is very severe even experienced anglers can fish all day without a bite. For this reason the winter can be a discouraging time to take up fishing.

You will also learn that fish are not scattered evenly throughout a water. Some spots (called 'pitches' in stillwaters, or 'swims' in a river) are consistently better than others. The best spots might well be near weedbeds or where the depth changes suddenly. Depths can be found by using a float and plummet. Do not try to keep the information obtained in this way in your head — you will almost certainly forget it. It is far better to make simple sketch maps.

Do not assume that the best places to fish will necessarily be the most comfortable places. Sometimes it is a good idea to explore out-of-the-way pitches that are ignored by other anglers.

Remember at all times that a fish is a wild creature — it is timid and very easily frightened. The angler who makes a lot of noise is not likely to be very successful. Some anglers are extremely heavy-footed and spoil their chances of sport as a result. When fishing you should tread lightly, try not to knock things over or drop things on the bank and never hammer rod-rests into hard ground. It is a good idea to sit well back from the water's edge too. If there is cover in the form of marginal reeds, use this to hide yourself from the fish. You will not catch fish that have been frightened by noise, vibration and movement, no matter how expensive your tackle or how good your bait.

As you gain in experience you will want to graduate to larger lakes and pits. Here you are likely to encounter much deeper water than you found in your small ponds — depths of 20 feet or more are by no means unusual. Deep water presents its own special problems and new techniques will have to be learnt to cope with the situation. Big waters are exposed to the wind as well, and you will find that wind sets water in motion, sometimes producing large waves. Results on big lakes and pits are likely to be disappointing at first, for they can be very difficult waters to fish, but with persistence the problems will be overcome and you find that these waters have their own very special attractions.

When you have mastered the basic skills of stillwater fishing you will doubtless want to try river fishing. Some of the methods you have used in stillwater will be of use on the river — but for consistent success you will need to learn about other methods too. Detailed descriptions of these various methods and tactics will be found in later chapters.

Canals and drains are, in effect, man-made rivers, and like rivers they vary tremendously in character. Some, especially the overgrown neglected ones, are virtually long, thin ponds. They have little or no flow and can be regarded as stillwaters. Some, like the drains of Fenland, often have quite a fast flow.

Finally, a few general words of advice. The successful angler needs to be a sound naturalist. Only by learning how fish behave can he hope to choose the best spots in a water and predict how they might feed. He needs to be something of an athlete, too, for there are many athletic skills in fishing, the most obvious of which is casting. A good caster can apparently effortlessly put his bait exactly where he wants it to go. The successful angler needs stamina to maintain concentration for long periods, sometimes in the most appalling weather conditions. He needs to have a retentive mind — there is so much to learn in fishing. But most of all he needs determination. You get out of fishing what you are prepared to put into it. If you are willing to work hard at your fishing and put a lot of effort into it, you will be more consistently successful than the man who treats the whole thing rather casually. Luck plays very little part in angling. It is estimated that ten per cent of anglers catch ninety per cent of the fish. If you are determined enough, you can become one of the successful ten per cent. It is up to you.

Tackle

Any newcomer to angling, confronted by the vast array of fishing tackle, must be left wondering how to make the correct choice of equipment. First one must consider which fishing approach to take: for most beginners the two main types will be float and leger fishing. A rod of about 12-13 feet and balanced with a fixed-spool reel carrying a line of $2\frac{1}{2}$ lb breaking strain form the main items in a basic outfit for float fishing, plus a selection of floats, some split shot in a dispenser and hooks in sizes 16 to 20 tied to hooklengths of $1\frac{1}{2}$-2 lb breaking strain. Even a youngster starting out for the first time should have a float rod at least 11 feet long to allow adequate tackle control from the beginning.

Leger tackle requires a shorter rod, around 10 feet in length, as bites will be indicated not by a float but by some form of bite indicator such as a swingtip, quivertip or springtip attached to the end of the rod. The reel should be loaded with a line of 3 lb breaking strain and hook sizes 14 to 18, with eyed hooks in sizes 8 to 12 if bigger baits are to be used. A weight of some form is required, so the popular Arlesey bomb or a group of swan shots will complete this broad outline of leger tackle.

It is important to understand from the start that rod, reel, line and hooks should be balanced so that they work with each other for the benefit of the angler. As an illustration of the effects of unbalanced tackle, a powerful carp rod used with a reel line of only 2 lb breaking strain would inevitably result in a broken line, either when casting or striking. On the other hand, reel line that is too strong and not matched to the rod will strain the rod, probably resulting in a broken top joint.

Similarly, a large hook such as a size 4 used in conjunction with a hooklength of only 1 lb breaking strain will mean a broken hooklength because more than 1 lb pressure is required to set the hook. A balanced outfit helps to open up the delights and pleasure of angling to a novice, giving every opportunity to hook and land the fish of a lifetime.

A common problem for beginners centres around the question of the correct tackle for particular waters. If the water holds only very big fish — around 5 lb or more — then a more specialist approach, possibly with leger tackle, and a rod cap-

The basic outfits for leger fishing (above) and float fishing (below).

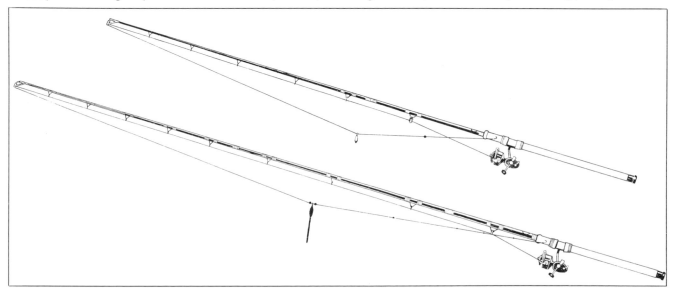

able of landing fish of this size will be necessary. A water containing small fish up to 1 lb in weight, with a sprinkling of larger fish up to about 4 lb, can be fished with general coarse fishing tackle. If a bigger fish is hooked it can be landed on this lighter gear but will take a little longer, adding to the thrill and excitement.

A canal or small pond holding very small fish requires a very delicate approach, especially if the water is clear. If the water has some colour, perhaps after heavy rain, then stronger tackle can be used as the fish will not be so easily scared.

Rods

Rods which have been designed for specific purposes demonstrate fundamental differences in their application, but consider first the tasks a rod has to perform. Broadly, these are casting, striking and playing a fish. The emphasis of the rod design is placed upon what is considered to be its most important function.

In a 'tip-action' match rod, with striking as its primary task, only the top section of the rod bends to any degree. This gives a very fast strike, enabling line to be picked up off the water very quickly. This type of rod is ideally suited to light float fishing on still or slow-moving waters.

The medium-action rod, a leger rod or a more general purpose float rod, has an action extending from the tip to about halfway down the rod, producing a strike effective over long distances. This rod is capable of tackling both small and somewhat larger fish.

A through-action rod bends throughout its entire length from the tip right through to the butt. This is a powerful rod designed for casting large baits and for playing big fish including carp, barbel, pike, and so on.

An indication of the 'power' of a rod can be derived from its 'test curve' which, quite simply, is the maximum amount of pressure the rod can apply. To check a test curve, hook a spring balance — preferably calibrated in ounces rather than pounds — to the reel line of the rod. The test curve is the amount of pull required to bend the rod into a quarter-circle. A rod with a 1 lb test curve would be ideally suited to hook-lengths of around $1\frac{1}{2}$-2 lb breaking strain. A test curve of some 2 lb would be just right for reel lines of around 8-10 lb.

Most rods are made from fibreglass, polyester compounds or carbon-fibre. All of these will have glass-to-glass ferrules. Rods with ferrules made from metal or from Spanish reed, Tonkin cane or a tubular steel construction are now somewhat dated. All float rods should have 'high bell' intermediate rings to prevent line sticking to the rod in wet conditions, and lined butt and end rings. If the intermediates are also lined so much the better. There should be approximately one intermediate ring for each foot of rod, with at least five of these rings on the top joint. If there are too few rings the line will produce sharp angles as it passes through them, eventually causing grooves which may fray or break the reel line at a critical moment.

Opposite A good tackle shop will offer a wide variety of fishing tackle and equipment which can be rather confusing at first. It is helpful if you have previously considered which approach to fishing you are intending to take.

Below The three basic types of rod action. From left to right: tip-action rod, medium-action rod, through-action rod.

Bottom Different types of rod ring.

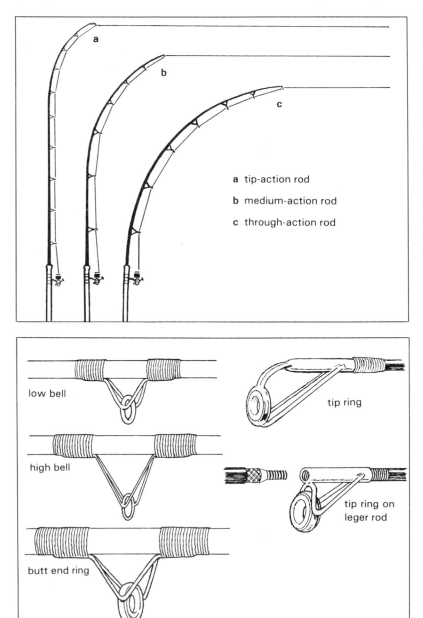

a tip-action rod

b medium-action rod

c through-action rod

low bell

high bell

butt end ring

tip ring

tip ring on leger rod

Rod rings should be small and light and yet as strong as possible to avoid upsetting the balance and action of the rod. Quality here is vital.

A screw-in end ring fitted to a 12 or 13 foot float rod to take a swingtip is a poor compromise, serving only to spoil its action. Sliding reel fittings are an advantage as they enable a reel to be placed in the best position to balance with the rod. It is important that a rod feels positive in the strike and suits the individual. A rod that feels tiring or top-heavy in the shop will be next to useless on the river bank.

Basic Rod Specifications

type	length (ft)	action	test curve	suggested reel lines	no. of sections
match rod	13	tip	12 oz	2-3 lb	3
general purpose float rod	12	medium	1 lb	$2\frac{1}{2}$-4 lb	3
leger rod	10	medium	$1\frac{1}{4}$ lb	3-5 lb	2
carp rod	10	through	2 lb	8-10 lb	2

Reels

The first choice for any beginner is the fixed-spool reel, as only a small amount of practice is needed to achieve long casts quite easily. The line is wound automatically on to a fixed spool by a bale arm that rotates around the spool as the handle is turned. Once the bale arm has been locked in the open position, as in casting, the line can flow freely from the top of the spool. Closing the bale arm, or placing a finger on the lip of the spool, prevents the release of more line.

A host of extras may tempt the would-be buyer, but there are several essential features that should be considered. A reel should always be smooth-running and as silent as possible, even with the anti-reverse mechanism on. Push-button release spools allow easy changes of reel spools with a minimum of fuss. Those with a system to prevent line going behind the spool are a great advantage. If the spare spool, normally supplied at the time of purchase, is extremely shallow and classed as a 'match' spool this should require no backing material to fill to the required depth, assuming that a line of 2-3 lb breaking strain is being used. Another useful feature is a line roller incorporated into the bale arm to prevent line and bale arm wear. For general coarse fishing a gear ratio of about $3\frac{1}{2}$-to-1 is quite adequate.

As rod and reel must be balanced it is always advisable to try them together inside, or even outside, the tackle shop.

Always position the reel about 6 inches below the top of the rod handle in order to get the correct rod/reel balance and so prevent the combination becoming too tiring during a long day's fishing. Two fingers placed either side of the reel stem

The three main types of coarse fishing reel.

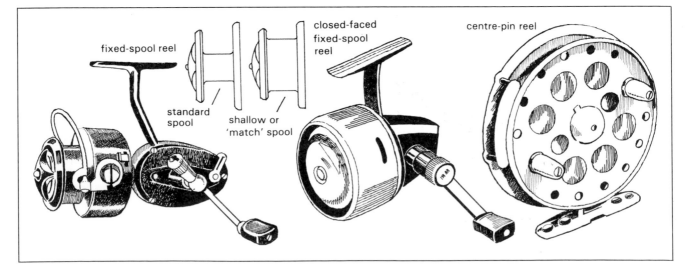

fixed-spool reel

standard spool

shallow or 'match' spool

closed-faced fixed-spool reel

centre-pin reel

will provide a comfortable grip on both rod and reel with the butt of the rod underneath the forearm. As the technique of feathering — slowing down the tackle in the air during casting — involves placing a finger on the lip of the spool, the fore or middle finger must be able to reach the top of the spool. Those with small fingers will probably need a smaller size of reel.

Left-hand wind or right-hand wind is a question that should always be asked but is often overlooked. If the rod is held in the right hand a left-hand wind reel is required and *vice versa*.

A closed-face reel has a particular advantage over fixed-spool reels in windy conditions because loose line cannot be blown back over the bale arm. This reduces considerably the chances of tangles at the reel itself. The spool is housed inside a cover and the line is wound on to it by a pick-up pin instead of a bale arm. Finger pressure on the button at the top of the spool releases the line.

A centre-pin reel was at one time the only reel available to anglers. It is now something of an expert's reel but is currently undergoing a revival on some rivers. A lot of practice is required to fish well with a centre-pin, which is basically a revolving drum. The pull of the water upon the tackle causes the drum to revolve and release line. Retrieving tackle quickly can be achieved with a technique known as 'batting'. The drum is struck or 'batted' by the palm of the hand during the retrieve.

Lines

Nylon lines are sold in spools holding 25, 50 or 100 yard lengths. Always load at least 100 yards on the reel spool so that any knots are completely buried and will not interfere with casting. Moreover, if any line is lost in the course of a day's fishing there will be plenty left to ensure that fishing can continue. As the line is used up knots will become visible and affect casting. When this happens, remove the old line as far as the knot and replace with a new 100-yard length. In any case, all lines deteriorate after a time and begin to lose strength, so it is a good idea to discard the first two yards of line as this will have been subjected to the greatest stress after being weakened by the float and shots. Do *not* leave discarded line on the river bank. Take it home and burn it.

Aim to fill the reel spool with line to

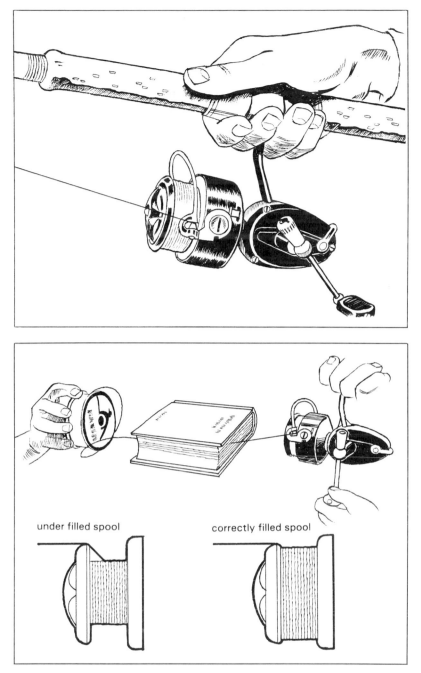

under filled spool   correctly filled spool

within $\frac{1}{16}$ inch of the spool lip so that line flows freely over the top. Overfilling will cause the line to fall off in loops, resulting in tangles. An under-loaded spool will restrict casting distance.

The correct way to load line on the spool is first to place the reel on the butt section of the rod. Remove the reel spool and tie the line to it by a simple double slip knot. Ask a friend to hold the back edge of the line spool. Replace the reel spool on the reel and close the bale arm. Commence to load the line by turning the reel handle. Apply a light tension to the line during loading by running it through the fingers. This prevents loose coils from developing.

Top Holding the reel with two fingers either side of the reel stem at about 6 inches below the top of the rod butt should provide a comfortable and balanced grip.

Above The correct way of loading line onto a fixed-spool reel entails holding the back edge of the line spool. A light tension to the line prevents loose coils developing.

All fishing lines are given a 'breaking strain', normally expressed in pounds, to indicate what load a line will take before it breaks. A useful range of lines is 2½ lb, 3 lb and 5 lb breaking strain for normal coarse fishing, remembering the need for a spare reel spool for each line. The 2½ lb line will serve for float fishing, 3 lb for legering and 5 lb held in reserve for both techniques under more difficult conditions, when fishing in very weedy swims or when big fish can be expected.

Using a line of 5 lb breaking strain does not mean that only fish up to 5 lb in weight may be landed. As a fish weighs less in the water, there is no reason why fish above the line breaking strain cannot be landed if played with care, provided rod and line are matched.

Look for dull, limp, smooth-surfaced and supple line. Avoid hard, shiny lines as these will often lie in coils upon the surface of the water or cause problems in casting. Obviously any line must be as fine as possible in diameter for a given breaking strain. This is because a fine line casts and fishes better, but it does not necessarily mean that the finest lines are the best. All lines stretch to some extent, giving a built-in safety factor if the strike has been too hard, so beware of any pre-stretched lines in which this safety factor has been removed.

More emphasis should be placed on fine-diameter lines when used for tying hooklengths as a coarse line will affect bait presentation. Line for making hooklengths can be purchased in 25 yard spools.

Line Guide

breaking strain (lbs)	diameter (ins)	possible use	probable species of fish
2·5	·005	general float fishing or light legering	roach, rudd, gudgeon, bleak, dace, bream, perch
3	·006	heavier float fishing and legering	chub, bream, tench
5	·009	float fishing in very weedy swims when fishing for specimen fish – legering in weedy swims or fast water	chub, bream, tench, barbel, small carp
10	·014	spinning for pike, stillwater legering for specimen fish	carp, pike, eels, barbel

Hooks

The size of a hook is easily determined by its number, but the size in relation to the number can cause confusion. For example, a high number such as a size 24 refers to a very tiny hook, while a low number such as size 8 indicates quite a large hook. The most common hook sizes in use for general coarse fishing are 16, 18 or 20 when maggots or casters are used for bait. Larger baits, such as worms or bread-flake, requires hook sizes around size 6 to 14. Extremely large hooks, 1 to 4, are used for specialist baits or where very big fish are being sought. In general, a big bait requires a big hook.

Eyed hooks are sold in most sizes down to a size 20 but they are best used in the larger sizes – 6 to 14 – when delicate presentation of the bait is not so important. These hooks are sold separately in packets of 10 or 100 and are tied to the line via the eye, using a special knot.

Spade-end hooks are particularly effective in the smaller sizes, i.e. 16 to 24, as they can be tied very neatly to fine lines using a simple but effective spade-end knot. They are sold in packets of 10, 50 or 100 and

A typical range of spade-end hooks shown actual size. Notice that the lower the figure the larger the hook.

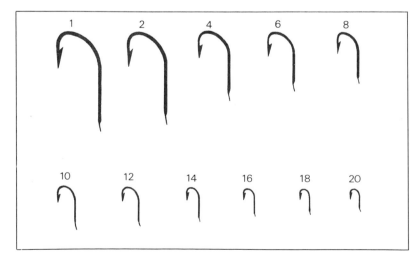

A collection of floats.

represent a real saving in cost if tied at home. The spade-end whipping knot is quite easy to learn.

It is important to match the breaking strain of a hooklength to the reel line and hook size. The breaking strain of a hooklength should always be lower than that of the main reel line, so that any breaks on the terminal tackle result only in the loss of hook and hooklength. As an example, a 2 lb reel line warrants a hooklength of about $1\frac{1}{2}$ lb or less.

It is equally important for small hooks to be tied to fine hooklengths in order to present the bait to the fish as naturally as possible. A coarse hooklength will seriously impair this delicate approach. Use a 1-$1\frac{1}{2}$ lb hooklength for a size 20 hook, $1\frac{1}{2}$-2 lb for an 18, and about 2-$2\frac{1}{2}$ lb for a size 16.

A complete beginner may prefer to purchase hooks already tied to nylon until the art of tying hooks has been mastered. These are always available at tackle shops, but they work out more expensive, especially if several of them are lost in a day's fishing.

Hook patterns available include several that have become extremely popular for specific angling techniques. A fine wire gilt hook (golden colour) is preferred by many when maggot fishing, especially when bronze maggot is used as a hook-bait. For caster fishing, when the hook is buried inside the bait, a long-shank fine wire hook is best. A short-shanked forged reverse hook, which has more strength than a fine wire hook, is a popular choice for bream fishing on most waters.

Floats

A popular misconception among new-comers to fishing is that just one float will do for all styles of float fishing and all types

Knots. Every angler needs to know a few simple knots for tying hooks and lengths of line. These are some simple knots which should be adequate for general use.

grinner (line to eyed hook)

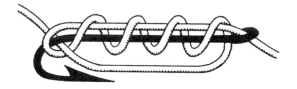

tucked half-blood (line to eyed or spade-end hook; tied along shank)

whipping (line to spade-end hook)

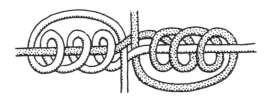

blood knot (line to line)

three turn loop knot

of water, whether canal, river, reservoir or gravel pit. A beginner often has a good catch of fish on a particular float and continues to use that same float over and over again, irrespective of the type of water being fished. This is the wrong approach.

In stillwaters, where the fish has plenty of time to examine the bait, a sensitive float with a very fine tip is a great advantage as it gives a more positive indication of a bite. A river or small sidestream with a turbulent flow requires a more buoyant float that can ride through the swim without being pulled under by the current.

It is always worth while to have three or even four floats of a particular type but which take different shot loads. This allows a change to a heavier float, which may be needed to retain full control of the tackle if conditions deteriorate.

An important point to establish at the start is the colour of float tip which suits you best. Orange and yellow are good but there are times when a black tip beats them all, especially if there are no reflections on the water. Steer clear of floats with brightly painted bodies. The best colours are black or dark green.

A recent innovation has been the printing of the shot-carrying capacity on the floats themselves by means of transfers. This gives a guide to the amount of shot required to cock the float correctly, but does not mean that only the shots appearing on the transfer should be used. If the transfer indicates 4AAA then the float could just as easily be shotted with 2AAA, 3BB, two No. 4 and a No. 8 (*see* Split shot).

When fishing close to the bank on running water, the float is best strapped to the line top and bottom with float rubbers. A stick float will be useful for conditions where the flow is gentle and the wind very light. More rugged conditions need one of the traditional Avon floats or a balsa float.

Distance fishing in still or slow-moving waters demands quite heavy floats which are attached to the line bottom end only. Peacock quill or Sarkandas reed 'wagglers', some with a balsa body at the base of the float, will be the order of the day. For somewhat shy bites either a cane antenna float or a cane insert waggler will be a useful asset.

A simple 'straight' waggler of peacock

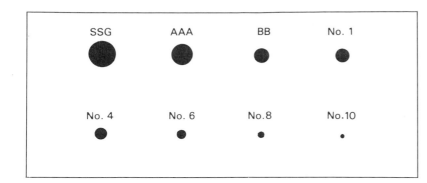

Above A selection of split shots showing the relative difference in size.

Below A tackle box with a wide range of compartments holding some of the angler's essential equipment such as split shot, spare spools of line, disgorgers, leger weights and bait droppers.

quill will perform very well indeed, both at a distance in running water or close in on still or slow-moving water, especially when 'laying-on'. Water and wind conditions influence the choice of float for the job in hand (*see* 'Float fishing' chapter).

Split shot

A sensible range of split shot to carry would be the following sizes: SSG, AAA, BB and Nos. 1, 4, 6 and 8 (dust shot), the

largest size being the SSG or swan shot, as it is often called. An approximate guide to the relationships between these shots is that two AAA shot equal one SSG and two BB shot equal one AAA. One BB shot is roughly equivalent to two No. 4, four No. 6 or eight No. 8.

Lead shots serve several purposes besides being used as weights to cock the float. If the shot are placed in a particular way or 'shotting pattern', different types of bite can be spotted more easily and the bait presented to the fish in a variety of ways. As the amount of shot the float takes will determine the distance out that can be fished, the rule of thumb is to be able to cast with ease to the farthest point in a swim without forcing the tackle out.

A bunch of weights placed nearer to the hook than the float is often referred to as bulk shot and will get the hookbait down to the bottom very quickly. Conversely, a small shot, for example a No. 8, placed near to the hook, if it is the only shot on the

terminal tackle will produce a slow drop of the hookbait throughout the entire depth of the swim.

If the reel line has been threaded through the float ring, then a shot placed on either side of the ring will prevent the float moving up or down the line. It is always a good idea to put a shot underneath the float to prevent it slipping if it has been attached to the line by two rubbers.

Lead shot are obtainable in individual packets or tubs containing only one size of shot or in round plastic dispensers with transparent revolving lids containing shot of varying sizes. Always buy the softest shot available. These ensure speedy changes of shot; hard shot often prove difficult to move easily, and may eventually damage fine lines. In general, the larger shots are placed near to the float. tapering down to the smallest shots nearest the hook.

To place a shot on the line simply put the line in the 'vee' of the shot and then gently squeeze the shot on to the line. The shot can be taken off by inserting a thumb-nail in the 'vee' but a penknife comes in useful for removing any really stubborn shots.

Legering, as a form of fishing without a float, requires its own specialised set of weights. The most widely used of these is the Arlesey bomb, a pear-shaped lead with a swivel at the top. Buying these in $\frac{1}{4}$ oz, $\frac{3}{8}$ oz and $\frac{1}{2}$ oz sizes should enable you to

Jim Gibbinson unhooking a fine roach using a pair of artery forceps.

This angler has his tackle and bait arranged so that he is able to see at a glance where everything is, and can therefore concentrate on his fishing.

cope with most situations. Other popular leger weights include coffin leads, barrel leads and drilled bullets, all available in differing weights and sizes. An alternative to the Arlesey bomb is a bunch of three or four swan shots on a short link, and this is as good as anything.

Essential accessories

A **basket** serves both as a seat and a carrying case for all those smaller items of tackle such as reels, float boxes, bait tins and so on. The traditional cane basket is fast being replaced by fibreglass tackle seats. Cane baskets are available in many sizes but the choice in fibreglass is somewhat restricted. Always buy a basket that will carry all your kit and a little more besides, as most anglers have a tendency to build up their tackle over the years.

You will also need a **rod holdall,** preferably containing plastic tubes to provide extra protection for your rods. Make sure the holdall incorporates at least a couple of pockets which are roomy enough to accommodate an umbrella and rod rests. Buy the biggest span **umbrella** you can afford – the extra weight and cost is negligible when compared with the misery of crouching beneath inadequate shelter which makes it impossible to fish efficiently through inclement weather.

Take a **catapult** to hard-fished waters where the fish are always some distance from the bank. This is absolutely indispensable for getting helpings of loose feed or groundbait out to where the fish are. The elastic should be between $\frac{1}{8}$ and $\frac{3}{16}$ inch square and have plenty of stretch. Avoid heavy cups, plastic or rubber, as these will reduce distance and accuracy. A soft leather pouch for loose feed and a leather pouch with a plastic cup for soft groundbaits will be ideal for long distances.

A **disgorger** will be required if the fish is hooked inside the mouth as opposed to being lip-hooked. The slit barrel type is slid down to the hook via the line. If bigger fish are the target or large hooks (around size 10 upwards) are being used, surgical or **artery forceps** are better.

Rod rests are required for more static forms of angling such as laying-on or legering, or just to hold the rod while you are unhooking the fish or rebaiting the hook. At least two rod rests are required for legering.

Sundries

There are several very small items that are always worth carrying on a fishing trip.
* **Float rubbers** of varying sizes or **silicon tubing** to attach a float to the reel line.
* **Plummet** for establishing the depth of a swim.

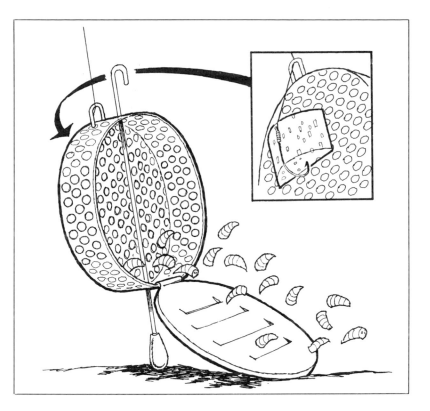

* **Small screwdriver** for on-the-spot reel repairs.
* **Scissors** for cutting or trimming the line.
* **Penknife** for removing stubborn shots.
* **Towel** for cleaning hands and items of tackle.
* **Plastic bowl** for mixing groundbait.
* **Plastic bait boxes** in 1 or 2 pint sizes.

A **tackle box** stores all those little odds and ends.

A bait dropper resting on the bottom with the lid open, releasing its contents. This method of swim feeding provides an accurate method of placing the feed. It should be carefully lowered over the area you are intending to fish either by a rod or a pole; it should not be cast.

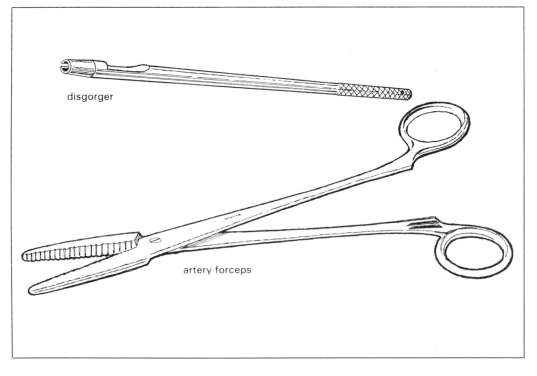

disgorger

artery forceps

A disgorger and a pair of artery forceps. A disgorger is useful if the fish has been hooked inside the mouth and the hook cannot be easily removed by hand. Artery forceps can be used when dealing with bigger fish.

Float fishing

A float permits the angler to present his bait at any depth in the water from just below the surface to right on the bottom in both rivers and stillwaters. When fishing a river, a float, if correctly weighted and properly controlled, can send a bait through the water in exactly the manner a fish might be expected to find its natural food. Also when fishing a bait on the bottom a float can either hold it still, permit it to travel along at a speed at which the current would carry an unattached bait or, if the angler considers it necessary, faster or slower than a fish would expect it to travel.

In stillwaters, where the fish are often to be found feeding off the bottom, the use of a float will allow the bait to fall slowly through the water. The manner in which the shots are attached to the line will further determine how fast or slow it falls. The bait also affects the rate of descent; for instance, sweetcorn will sink faster than a single maggot or a piece of flake. When on the bottom in stillwaters, the bait should remain still and in order to achieve this the float should be attached bottom end only.

At one time the most common float in use was the porcupine quill which seemed to suffice for whatever species was sought. However, times have changed and today the range of floats available is so vast that the average angler, and certainly the newcomer, is often bemused by them all. This proliferation of floats largely stems from the search for more sophisticated methods of bite detection and bait presentation to help maintain sporting success whatever the water and weather.

Let us look at seven types of float in general use, starting with the antennas which include the **windbeaters**. These are stillwater floats designed to remain stable in windy conditions. Each pattern has a long antenna with a fairly weighty body and a ring on the bottom. On the top of the windbeater antenna is a 'sight bob' which is usually made of polystyrene. The float is attached to the line at the base only. When using a windbeater — or any antenna for that matter — it is important to follow the correct shotting pattern. A large shot goes immediately below the windbeater float, with an AAA about 15 inches above the hook with the rest of the shot grouped

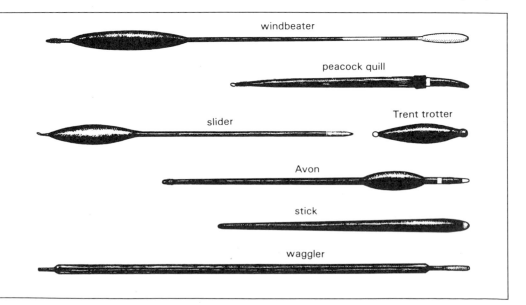

A selection of popular floats used by coarse anglers.

windbeater

peacock quill

slider

Trent trotter

Avon

stick

waggler

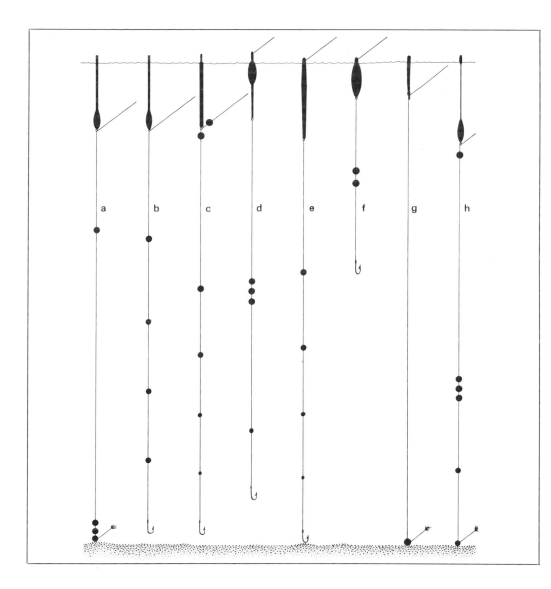

Recommended shotting patterns for seven types of float: **a** slider pattern for fishing on the bottom, **b** slider pattern for fishing on the drop, **c** waggler, **d** Avon, **e** stick, **f** Trent trotter, **g** peacock quill pattern for lift method, **h** windbeater.

about 12 inches above that. Finally a BB shot (in a strong wind or drift an AAA is better) is placed about 3 inches from the hook and should rest on the bottom. After the bait is cast and the BB shot is resting on the bottom the line is sunk by thrusting the rod tip under the water by about 2 feet and reeling the line taut between rod tip and float. The rod is then placed on two rod rests with 2 inches of the tip still submerged. If the float has been weighted correctly only the sight bob will show above the surface. Bites are usually indicated when the fish lifts that all-important bottom shot causing part of the antenna to rise. This is usually followed by both the antenna and the sight bob sinking out of sight. The windbeater is not a float for fishing a bait off the bottom as at all times the BB shot must rest on the bottom. Also the line must be completely sunk.

One of the finest methods of stillwater fishing with a big bait (like crust or worm)

is called the 'lift'. Here, a length of peacock quill of about 4-5 inches is attached at its base to the line using a float rubber with one swan shot pinched on the line about 2 inches from the bait. As when fishing with a windbeater both the rod tip and line are submerged. There should not be more than 1 inch of quill above the surface of the water. Bites are indicated by the quill suddenly rising and lying flat (as the fish lifts the shot) and sometimes shooting under immediately afterwards.

The **'Trent Trotter'** is a small dumpy float which takes a fair amount of shot for its size. It is a handy float, especially for fishing with subsurface baits as when chub fishing with bread just beneath the surface. The float is attached at the tip and base ('fished double rubber') and set 2-3 feet from the hook. The weights, which usually consist of one or two swan shots, are placed about halfway between the float and the bait. As there is only a little of the float above the surface, the float usually disappears when a fish takes the bait. The 'Trotter' is also effective when seeking rudd at subsurface, and sometimes also big roach. At all times the line must float.

The **stick float** is a river float for close-range fishing in waters of medium flow with small baits on fine tackle. Stick floats are usually made from two-thirds cane and one-third balsa, the top half being slightly stouter than the bottom; the float is 'fished double rubber' on lines no heavier than 4 lb breaking strain. The shotting pattern with this float is important: the shots should be evenly spaced between the float and the hook, starting with the biggest nearest the float and graduating down to the smallest nearest the hook, which should be about 12 inches away from the lowest shot. The float is shotted so that no more than $\frac{1}{4}$ inch is above the surface.

The cast is made slightly upstream of the angler with the line taut to the float as it travels downriver, this is called 'trotting'. At the end of the swim, the float is checked slightly and held there, causing the bait to rise. Bites usually occur during the run-through or whilst the bait is rising. Because so little of the float is showing, most bites result in the float disappearing completely. The stick should never be used in fast-flowing water, in a downstream wind, or further out from the bank than you can cast underarm, otherwise control will be lost.

The **Avon** float is a good general river float with a fairly stout tip which carries a fair amount of weight and is ideal for anyone to serve their 'apprenticeship' on. Avons vary in size and shot-loading but a good one to start with would be about 6 inches in length with a shot-loading of about six AAA. The bottom shot (a BB) is placed anywhere between 5 and 18 inches from the hook. When maggots, bread or worms are used the rest of the shot should be grouped about halfway between the hook and the float. It is fished double rubber and, like the stick, is trotted then held back.

The **waggler** is generally associated with match fishing, but once the reader has become proficient with the Avon he should learn to use the waggler as it has several advantages over other floats. The waggler is a slim float which is uniform in diameter throughout except the tip, which has a short but fine antenna. Its primary function is for fishing maggots, casters and hemp on fine tackle (for example, 2 lb breaking strain reel line with 1 lb hooklength) but you need not be restricted to these three baits, nor such fine lines. The float is fished bottom only and is locked in position not by a length of rubber but by two shots, one either side of the ring at the base of the float. This not only ensures that the float 'rides' the water correctly but permits long, accurate casts — for which the waggler was originally intended.

On some large rivers big bags of chub

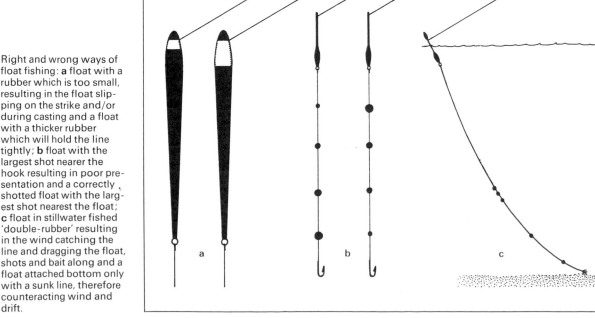

Right and wrong ways of float fishing: **a** float with a rubber which is too small, resulting in the float slipping on the strike and/or during casting and a float with a thicker rubber which will hold the line tightly; **b** float with the largest shot nearer the hook resulting in poor presentation and a correctly shotted float with the largest shot nearest the float; **c** float in stillwater fished 'double-rubber' resulting in the wind catching the line and dragging the float, shots and bait along and a float attached bottom only with a sunk line, therefore counteracting wind and drift.

are regularly taken by fishing against the far bank and as this can be 20-30 yards away a float which travels through the air like a dart is essential. The waggler is also used when bream fishing at long range. The remainder of the shots are spread down the line, grading to the smallest which should be about 15 inches above the hook.

The waggler is cast overhead, the line being slightly checked immediately before the tackle touches the water to ensure the line between the float and the bait does not fall in a heap. The float should land slightly downstream of the angler. Next, the rod tip is lowered to assist the line in sinking, but do not worry if a 'bow' forms immediately in front of the float before it sinks. Many anglers consider this an advantage. The strike — actually this is a misnomer, a 'pull' would be more accurate, especially when using fine tackle — is made sideways with the rod still held low. Because the line is sunk, the waggler is much less affected by wind than other floats and is therefore an important float in the angler's armoury.

When fishing very deep water (12 feet and over) in stillwater, a **sliding float** can be easier to fish with than a fixed one. Many floats can be used as sliders but it is essential that the inside diameter of the ring at the base is no more than $\frac{1}{3}$ inch. A float which carries a fair amount of shot is essential, otherwise difficulty will be experienced in getting it to work effectively. A shot-loading of two swans or more will do the trick.

An important feature is a stop knot which is tied on the line above the float at the required distance from the hook as shown above. Use a piece of line about 8 inches long to tie this knot. When pulled tight it can be slid along the line, but make sure the line is tight otherwise a kink can develop. Trim the ends of the knot to within $\frac{1}{8}$ inch. Do not use a reel line lighter than 3 lb when fishing with a slider otherwise you run the risk of smashing up on the strike.

The line is passed through the ring at the base of the float. If fishing 'on the drop' the shots should be spread evenly; if fishing on the bottom, they should be grouped together. The hook is then attached to a plummet. If the float disappears pull the stop knot further up the line and continue moving the knot and plumb until the float

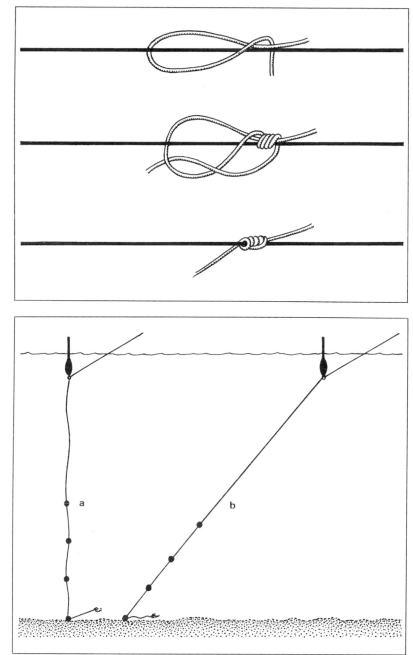

stands upright. The shot nearest the float should be about 5 feet from the hook; if it is less than this difficulty may be experienced in getting the float, which rests against this shot during casting, to slide up the line quickly enough. As the float hits the water the line must be kept slack. If this is not done the line between the float and the hook will be at an angle instead of vertical. When the bait is in position, the line is sunk and the rod, supported by two rests, should have the tip submerged.

When float fishing, if you are to present the bait correctly it is vital that you know the depth of your swim and the contours surrounding it. You can determine this by continual casting and adjustment of the

Top A sliding float stop knot.

Above A sliding float in the right and wrong positions: **a** float has run up a slack line; **b** float has run up a tight line.

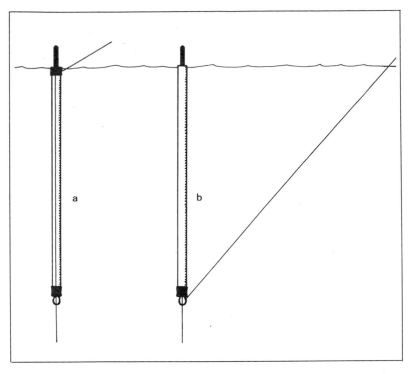

Methods of line attachment in floats: **a** float attached 'double-rubber'; **b** float attached bottom only.

Left Plumbing the bottom: **a** exactly the right depth; **b** float set too deep; **c** float set too shallow.
Right Two types of plummet: **a** plummet with cork in the base; **b** plummet with jaws which are fastened around the hook.

float sinks, push it up further until it lies flat on the surface, then push it down a little until the tip just shows above the surface. Now cast a little to the left, then to the right, then outwards, then inwards until you have formed a mental picture of the contours in and around your swim. Do not cast overhead, as this will result in the plummet hitting the water with a splash. It is better to cast gently and little disturbance will ensue.

You now know your bait will be on the bottom. If you are fishing a river, 'trot' your bait through the swim for half an hour or so and see what happens. If nothing does, then it is time to start experimenting.

First, pull the float down a couple of inches (so that the bait is off the bottom) and trot the float through again several times. If there is no result, push it down another 12 inches and try again, then push it down yet another 12 inches if there continues to be no response. Should this not produce a bite push the float back up to its original position, then a further 6 inches. You are now fishing over-depth. Cast so the float lands about 4 feet further over, past the 'line' of your swim, then with the rod held high so the line is clear of the water, allow the float and bait to roll round through the line of your swim until it is about 3 feet to your side of it. If nothing results, repeat this procedure, but this time further down the swim. Try this several times, each time casting further downstream. If you still have not had any bites then push the float up another 6 inches

float position until the float lies flat (when it is set too deep), but this method does not tell you much about any depressions or 'hills' which may be nearby. The use of a plummet will enable you to map out a more complete picture. The best plummets are those with a piece of cork in the base. With these the hook is passed through the ring at the top of the plummet then stuck into the cork. Some models have jaws which open and close by means of a spring. These are clipped on the hook. Having attached the plummet, push the float up, say, 7 feet from the hook, and cast. If the

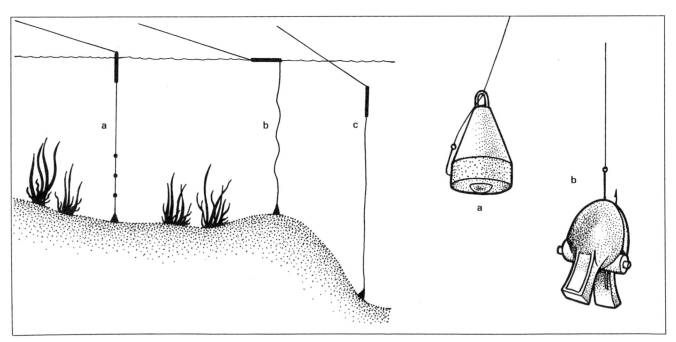

and cast into the line of your swim and, with the rod held high, hold the float in that position. It should now lie at half-cock. This is called 'laying-on'. Every two minutes gently raise the rod so the float and bait move a few inches, and so on.

In stillwaters you will invariably start with the bait on the bottom. Should no bites result, experiment by adjusting the shots so the bait falls gently through the water eventually finishing on the bottom.

The nature of the 'swim', the bushes or the trees immediately surrounding you and the method you are adopting will, most times, determine whether the cast is made overhead, sideways or underarm. But a windbeater float will fly better when cast overhead, whereas a stick float should be cast sideways.

Whether the cast is a two-handed affair or one-handed can depend on the technique adopted – for an overhead cast use two hands; for a sideways or underarm, one hand. However you cast, at all times the following sequence must be observed:

with the float hanging below the rod, lift the bale arm off the reel and trap the line with one finger of your casting arm.

If casting overhead take the rod back to about a 2 o'clock position with one finger still on the spool, the other hand gripping the rod handle about 18 inches below the reel. Bring the rod forward, then, as it reaches a 10 o'clock position, lift your finger off the spool.

For a sideways cast the rod is held with one hand, again with one finger on the spool but this time with the tip of the rod at about shoulder height. Again, start from a 2 o'clock position finishing at 10 o'clock.

The underarm cast can again be carried out with one hand and is used only where the float is cast relatively close to the near bank. For this method you hold the rod directly in front, then gently swing the rod top upwards releasing the finger from the spool after the rod top has travelled about 2 feet. For all casting it is important that you have the float under control immediately it is in the water. The method by

Casting with float tackle and a closed-face reel.

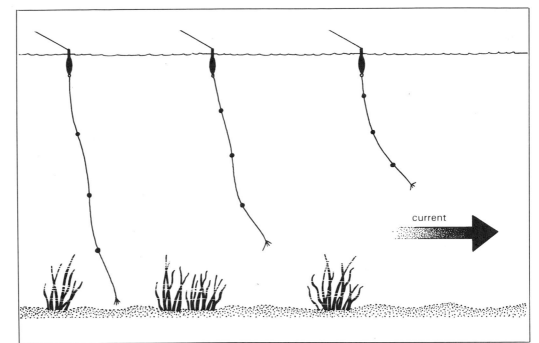

current

Right Laying-on is a good method of presenting a stationary bait when float fishing a river. When using this approach the bait must be fished over-depth.

Below If you wish the bait to move across the line of the swim you should cast over the swim and, holding the rod high so that the line is clear of the water, allow the bait to roll through the swim.

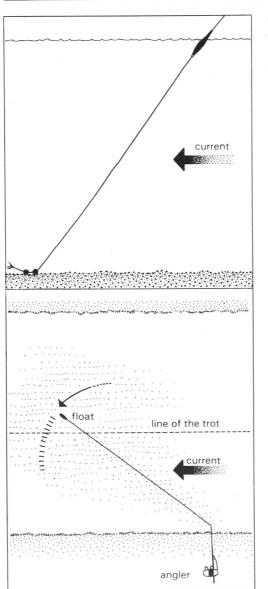

current

line of the trot

float

current

angler

Opposite top When fishing stillwaters with the bait on the bottom it is possible to let the bait fall gently through the water by adjusting the shots more evenly. This is called fishing 'on the drop'.

Opposite bottom When 'trotting' on a river you can prevent a bow from forming in the line by rolling the rod tip in the opposite direction to the current. This is called 'mending' the line.

which this is done depends on your situation and approach. For river fishing, if you are laying-on close in, immediately the bait sinks and the float 'cocks' take up any slack line until it is taut to the float. The rod is either held, or supported by two rests. For this the bale arm is closed.

When trotting close in, immediately the float cocks make sure the line is straight between rod tip and float. As the float travels downriver, release line from the spool by lifting one finger from the spool, trapping it again should a bow in the line appear. The bale arm is left open.

When trotting with the float across river (that is, with the float well out from the bank but still travelling downriver) care must be taken to prevent a bow in the line developing which will pull the float round and affect the presentation of the bait. This is called 'mending the line'. Immediately a bow in the line appears, lift the rod tip and flick it back in the opposite direction to that which the float is travelling. The slack line you pick up will remain on the water but this, if you have mended in good time, i.e. before the bow develops, should not be so much that it will affect the strike. Should too much slack line develop after mending has taken place, give the reel handle a few turns. If the trot is started slightly upstream of where you are sitting and is not intended to carry on too far, the bale arm can be closed. If required, more line can be given by opening the bale-arm then closing it again. For long trots it should be left open as previously described.

Whether the strike is made upwards or sideways depends again on your approach. If trotting well across river with the float almost in front of you, strike upwards. However, if the float is at a 90 degree angle to the rod tip, it is best to strike sideways.

In stillwaters the bale arm is closed, but whether the rod is held or supported is a matter of preference. Where quick or minute bites are expected the rod is best held, but where more positive and slower bites are expected it is best supported. Immediately the float cocks after casting plunge the rod tip under water up to about 2 feet, at the same time gently taking up any slack line, then leave about 2-3 inches of the rod tip submerged whilst fishing. For this type of fishing, at all times the strike is made upwards, the only exception being when swing-tipping with the rod parallel to the bank; then the strike is made sideways.

Having hooked the fish the important point to remember at all times is to keep the line taut. If the fish is small it is simply lifted from the water, but if it is of any size it must be played.

Before you start fishing, the clutch of the fixed spool must be correctly set. In order to do this catch hold of the line after it has been threaded through the rings and pull until the rod tip is at an angle of 90 degrees. At this point the clutch should slip; if it does not, slightly loosen the tension nut. Alternatively, if the clutch slips before the 90 degree angle is reached, tighten it.

After you have made a strike you start to retrieve the line with one finger just touching the rim of the spool. However, you do not just wind in, you 'pump'. With the rod pointing slightly skywards (never straight) pull the rod back gently, with one finger lightly on the rim of the spool. As the rod nears the 12 o'clock position you gently lower it to just before 10 o'clock, simultaneously winding in; then take the rod back again and repeat the action, and so on. Remember that when you lower the rod, *always* wind in, and keep the line tight.

If the fish should bolt, and takes line, keep the rod at 12 o'clock and let it take line from the clutch with one finger always on the rim of the spool. Just how much line the fish takes is controlled by that finger increasing pressure on the spool. If the fish begins to pull the rod forward, slightly release the finger pressure. When the fish is no longer taking line you can begin to retrieve.

Finally the fish is within netting distance. You should then place the net in the water, or if possible a little before this, then push your finger down hard on the spool and bring the rod back over your shoulder.

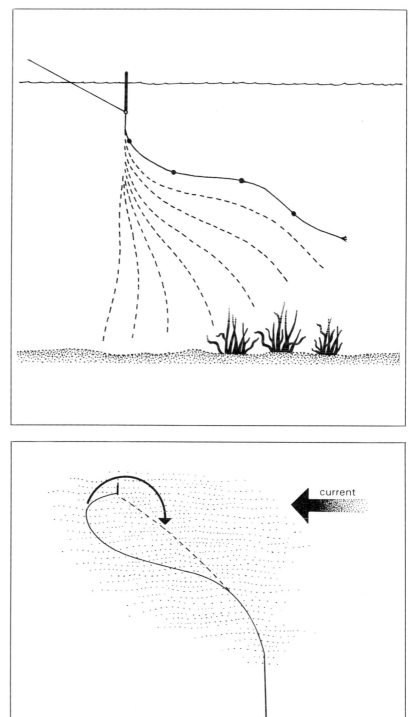

current

angler

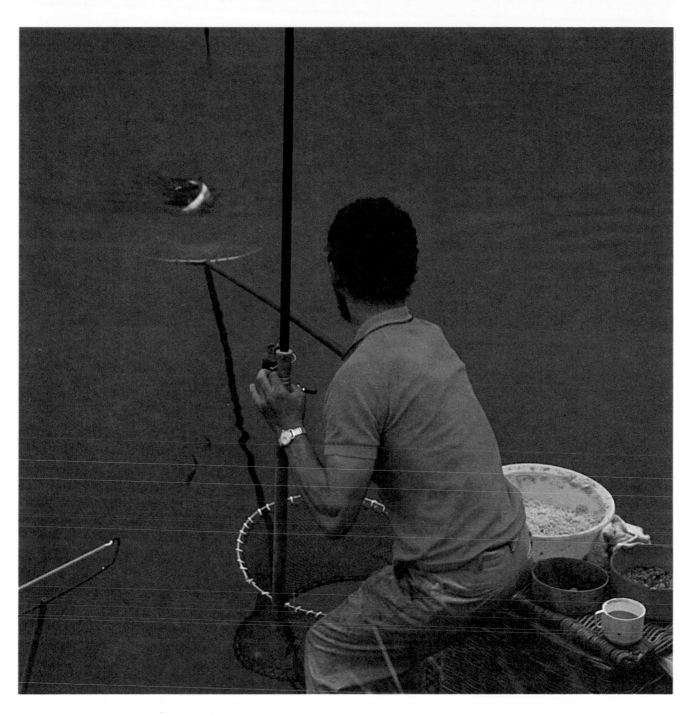

If you have done everything right the fish should slide over the net with the rod at between 1 and 2 o'clock. If with the rod back this far the fish has not reached the net, do not pull the rod back further but recover more line then start again. Wait until the fish is right over the submerged net before you lift and *never* attempt to net fish by pushing it forward.

Having got the fish on the bank, dip your hand in the water and grip it firmly immediately behind the head. Do not press on its gill covers. If the hook is only just inside its mouth it can be removed by hand, but if further down some kind of aid will be necessary. Disgorgers are useful, but avoid using the pronged variety which can cause damage. A good pair of artery forceps is better. Remove the hook gently by pushing and turning.

Once you have mastered the technique of controlling the line and getting the float to 'go through' properly (so it does not affect the bait presentation) waggler and stick fishing will come much more easily. Presenting a float in stillwater, though not simple, is not so difficult as river fishing, and a sophisticated float like a windbeater can be used with confidence almost immediately.

Above Angler showing the correct way of landing a fish with the fish about to be drawn over the submerged landing net.

Opposite A match angler about to land a fish caught on float fishing tackle.

Leger fishing

The technique of legering dispenses with the float, and the bait is usually anchored on the bottom by means of a single leger weight such as the Arlesey bomb. The bites are signalled on an indicator. These range from the swingtip to a simple bobbin suspended on the line between the reel and first ring.

Various factors determine which method of bite indication is best; for example, still or running water; finicky or bold bites, and the depth of the swim.

Legering has several advantages over float fishing. In particular it allows the angler to fish at distances far greater than with a float. Also it permits a stationary bait to be offered in fast water. Legering is not necessarily more deadly than float fishing, it is simply another way of catching fish. Days nevertheless occur when due to various factors such as strong winds, fast-flowing currents or distance, float fishing is either impossible or extremely difficult. On such days legering is the method most likely to succeed.

For instance, you may be fishing a river where the fish are feeding against the far bank 30 yards away. A competent angler can quite easily fish a float at that distance; but if a strong wind blowing into your face makes casting difficult, you leger. On some days it may not be the *best* way of presenting a bait, but the *only* one. To take another example, on stillwaters where the fish are feeding maybe 25 yards from the bank in 14 feet of water and there is little or no wind, a bait fished under a float may prove the best method. But if a strong facing or side wind renders float fishing impossible, again you leger. There are many other examples.

Like all methods, however, legering has its disadvantages. Days occur when river fish will only take a bait which is moving, say, 5 feet off the bottom. On such days it may be possible, by using a weight light enough not to hold bottom, in conjunction with a buoyant bait, to catch fish by legering. Yet the presentation would not be perfect: you might catch fish, but only in spite of and not because of it.

There are also days when the fish will only take a bait which is falling slowly through the water. The best method, if conditions allow, is to float fish adjusting the shots so the bait falls in a natural manner. Nevertheless, a falling bait can be presented on leger tackle. The length of line between lead and bait may of necessity be quite long — 5 feet — but the fish may be feeding more than 5 feet off the bottom and a longer 'tail' will be needed which can present all sorts of problems, especially for less experienced anglers.

One of the cheapest and most popular methods of legering is the sliding link, where the weights — usually swan shots — are attached to a separate length of nylon looped around the main line. The two main advantages of this rig are first that shots can be added or taken off to suit the speed of the current, and secondly that if the breaking strain of the link is lower than that of the main line, should the lead become snagged the link will break before the main line. If a lower breaking strain is not used and no knot is tied at the end of the link, the shots, if snagged, will pull off.

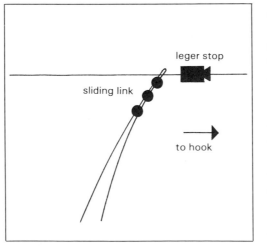

leger stop

sliding link

to hook

A sliding link is an inexpensive and flexible way of weighting a line. It is held in position here by a plastic leger stop.

Sometimes the fish are more responsive if the bait (and lead) roll, although only slightly, and to achieve this the amount of weight needed is critical. If a sliding link is used shots can be added or removed and the amount of weight can be adjusted to very fine limits indeed.

When a stationary bait is best, in waters of medium flow (where, say, $\frac{1}{2}$ oz will hold bottom) swan shots on a sliding link will suffice. In very fast water, however, where perhaps $\frac{3}{4}$ oz or over is necessary, a different set-up is better. A good lead for holding the bottom tightly is the coffin, an old-fashioned lead with a hole in the middle through which the line is threaded. However, any lead through which the line passes will, most days, result in bites being difficult to hit; so it is better to modify the coffin by pushing a swivel halfway into one of the holes then tapping it hard with a hammer. The line is then threaded through the swivel.

An alternative is to use swan shots on a sliding link, spread about an inch apart instead of being bunched. A number of shots spread will hold bottom where the same number bunched will not. The disadvantage with this method is the likelihood of tangling during casting. Overcome this by casting overhead and slightly checking the line immediately prior to the lead hitting the water.

There are several ways to stop the link or lead sliding down to the hook, including the plastic leger stop. This consists of a tiny plastic tube and a tapered pin. The line is threaded through the tube and held in position at the desired distance by the tapered pin. Push the pin in firmly. If you wish to move it do not attempt to push it up the line, but loosen the pin with artery forceps.

Split shot are *not* recommended as stoppers; they are not only prone to slipping on the strike but can also damage the line.

In stillwaters where bottom weed makes presentation difficult a paternoster is recommended. The main line is tied to the top of a 3-way swivel; another length of line (the length depending on how far you wish to fish the bait off bottom) is tied to the bottom, with the lead (usually an Arlesey bomb) attached to the end. A third length of nylon about 10 inches in length and with the hook attached is then tied to the remaining swivel eye.

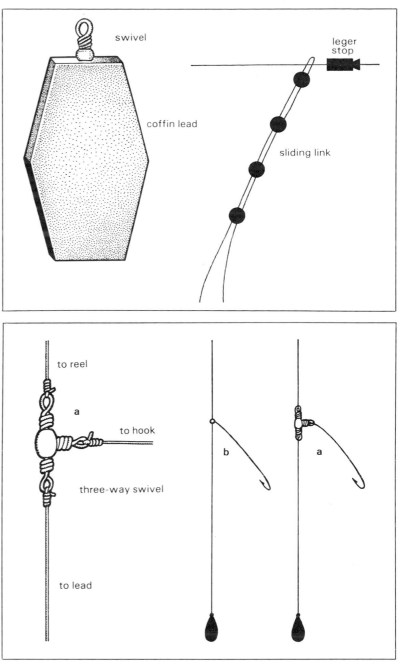

The paternoster is often effective in running water too. Some anglers, especially matchmen, make their paternosters in a different way, dispensing with the 3-way swivel. The hook is attached to a length of looped nylon which in turn is attached to the main line. Do this by forming a loop in the line, then placing the loop on the hooklength over it and passing the hook through both loops. BB shot at the bottom of the loop will prevent the hooklength slipping either on the strike or during playing of the fish. How far up the main line the hooklength is attached depends on how far you intend fishing the bait off the bottom. The Arlesey bomb is tied to the end of the main line.

Top A coffin lead with a swivel pushed halfway into the hole. The sliding link has swan shots evenly spread along its length which will enable it to hold the bottom more effectively in faster flowing waters.

Above A paternoster rig using (a) a three-way swivel and (b) a simple loop knot (method shown overleaf).

41

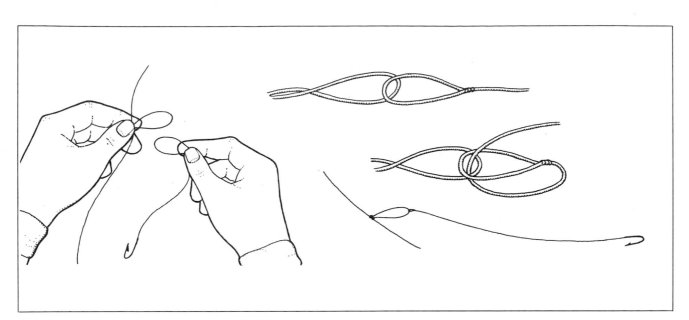

Method of attaching a looped hooklength to a loop in the reel line forming a paternoster.

Another rig consists of a line passed through the swivel eye of an Arlesey and stopped by a leger stop the required distance from the hook. One disadvantage with this method is that there is quite a difference in weight between the different bomb sizes and should a lighter or heavier one be necessary it means a complete breakdown of the tackle.

In situations where just one swan shot is necessary to hold or roll bottom, the shot can simply be pinched on the line without bite detection or presentation being impaired.

During the last few years, swim and blockend feeders have become extremely popular. The difference between the two concerns the ends: those on the swim-feeder are open, those on the blockend are closed. Many different types of blockend are available and they are mostly used when fishing maggots, casters or hemp with loose feed in the feeder. The blockend is stopped the required distance from the hook by either a swivel or leger stop.

Generally speaking small hooks — 16, 18 and 20 fished on a fine bottom (1-2 lb breaking strain) — are necessary when maggots, casters or hemp are used. But newcomers are advised to bait two or three maggots on a number 14, attached to 3 or 4 lb line, with maggots or hemp in the blockend. This will help to eliminate tackle losses until more experience is gained. While this may not prove successful in hard-fished waters (which newcomers would in any case do well to avoid) it will certainly catch fish in most, especially in stillwaters where tench, bream and roach

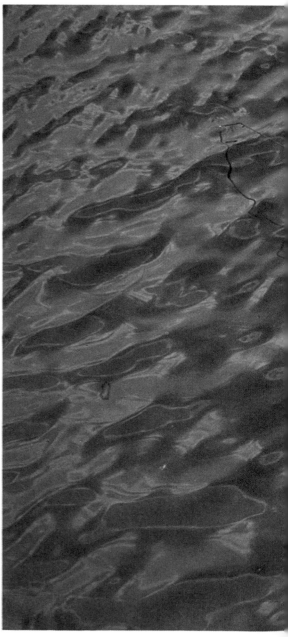

are the quarry. When using maggots in stillwaters always try to place the blockend in the same place each time you cast; this way you concentrate the fish and bites should come more regularly.

But you do not have to fish maggots, casters or hemp in conjunction with a blockend. In rivers holding a good head of chub, the bait can be luncheon meat, sausage meat or cheese paste fished on a number 12, 10 or 8 hook with a hooklength of approximately 15 inches. Some brands of luncheon meat tend to float however; if this happens reduce the 'tail' to about 8 inches. When fishing these baits with hemp in the blockend you should quickly bring the fish into the area, but as in stillwaters try to cast accurately.

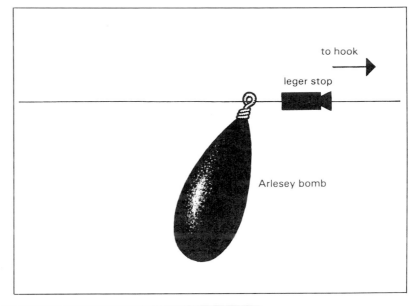

A leger rig with an Arlesey bomb on the main line with a plastic leger stop.

Angler legering for bream using a swingtip indicator.

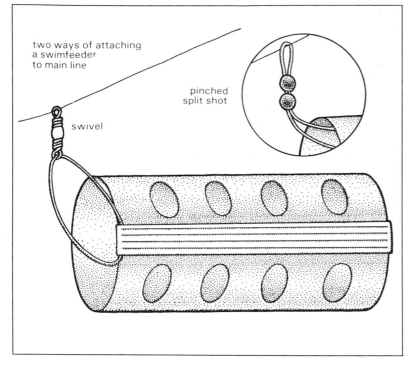

two ways of attaching a swimfeeder to main line

pinched split shot

swivel

A swimfeeder with a strip of lead along one side. These provide an efficient way of feeding the swim. These work best with a cereal groundbait.

The success of both blockends and swimfeeders is due almost entirely to the fact that the hookbait is always close to the groundbait or loose feed.

Swimfeeders, because the ends are open, are better suited to cereal groundbait. The mixture is important and should be such that it remains in the feeder during casting, but disintegrates immediately it reaches bottom. Here, as in many other things, practice makes perfect.

Swimfeeders are weighted by a strip of lead the length of the feeder and approximately $\frac{1}{2}$ inch wide. Some lead strips are stamped in three sizes: light, medium or heavy. These are worth seeking out as the correct weight swimfeeder can then be matched to the right conditions or strength of flow. Swimfeeders are useful when fishing with bread or worms and where a lot of cereal feed is necessary to hold the fish in the swim. Many anglers use them when bream fishing, but it is questionable whether sufficient groundbait can be introduced via a swimfeeder to contain a big shoal.

An important factor concerning tackle is the knots. Not only must the right knot be tied, it must be tied properly. Two trusted and popular knots are the tucked half-blood and the grinner. Make sure the line or hooklength is thick enough in relation to the hook eye, swivel or ring. Before pulling a knot tight, moisten it between your lips, then test it after pulling it tight.

Touch-legering is fast becoming a forgotten art, but it is a fine method of bite detection and should be learnt. Having cast out tuck the handle under your right arm, if possible with the rod top pointing downwards with the line just above the reel between the thumb and forefinger of your left hand. Bites are detected by a sudden change of tension on the line; it may tighten or slacken, but whatever it does you will feel it, and if you watch the top you will see it too. It is important to hold the rod still, and if you find this difficult you can support it on a rod rest about one-third of the way down, but make sure the design of the rest is such that the line cannot become trapped between it and the rod.

In fast water the rod should be held pointing skywards in order to keep as much line as possible out of the water, thus preventing the lead from rolling around too quickly.

Bite indicators which can be used in both still and running water fall into six categories: electric bite alarms, bobbins, swingtips, springtips, quivertips and butt indicators.

Electric bite alarms are used mainly in stillwaters and are operated by batteries. Most alarms have an antenna which, when moved by the line passing along it, triggers off the buzzer and/or light inside. The alarm is positioned either in front of or behind the front rod rest (some models act as a rest too) with the line passed over the antenna. The pick-up of the reel is either left open or closed depending upon the species being sought.

When a fish picks up the bait and moves off, the sound from the buzzer will be constant. Often, however, the fish does not move off, but will pick up the bait, pull it an inch or so, sometimes eject it and sometimes not. These bites are known as 'twitchers' and are signalled by short sharp bleeps.

Whether you strike at a twitcher or not depends upon the species being sought and the size of bait, among other factors. Experience will tell you when to strike; newcomers must experiment. Electric bite alarms may also be used in conjunction with a bobbin. The angler waits for the buzzer to bleep, then watches the bobbin.

Bobbins are used mainly in stillwaters and usually consist of a piece of cork about 1 inch in diameter with a hair grip inserted through the middle. Attached to the bobbin by the closed end of the hair grip is a length of loose cord, which in turn is attached to a peg stuck in the ground between the rod handle and butt ring. The rod is supported by two rests. After the bait has been cast and the line tightened to the lead the line is carefully tucked in the open end of the hair grip and the bobbin pulled down about 12 inches.

Bites are signalled when the bobbin moves up or down. If it moves up 10 inches or so without stopping, the fish is moving off with the bait and can be struck accordingly. If it moves up sharply an inch or so the fish may or may not have the bait in its mouth (or it may be a fish brushing against the line), but if it does this several times in quick succession it often suggests — especially when fishing maggots in a blockend — that the fish has the bait firmly in its mouth. Should the bobbin drop back, the fish has the bait in its mouth and is swimming towards you. As a substitute for a home-made bobbin you can also mould a small lump of groundbait or bread paste over the line which flicks safely free when the strike is made.

The most widely used bite indicator is the swingtip which is probably unrivalled for sensitivity. It has been modified many times in recent seasons and a range of materials are now used in its construction including solid glass, dowel, cane, light steel, fibreglass and more latterly sarkandas reed and even carbon-fibre. They come in a variety of lengths to counteract differing conditions and depths and are screwed into the tip of the leger rod with a sleeve of rubber tubing providing the all-important flexibility between the screw fitting and the tip itself (see overleaf). Nowadays most tackle shops boast an excellent range of swingtips and if you choose a model which is approved by a leading match angler you should not go far wrong. But remember that a light bomb and long tip — or conversely a heavy bomb and short tip — almost guarantee tangles! Check with your tackle dealer to make sure

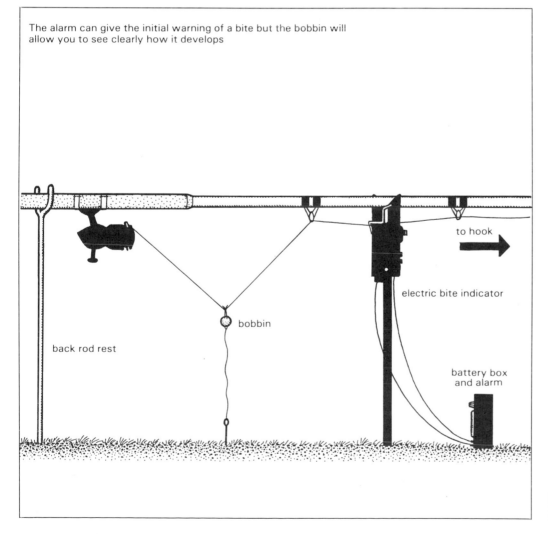

The alarm can give the initial warning of a bite but the bobbin will allow you to see clearly how it develops

to hook

electric bite indicator

bobbin

back rod rest

battery box and alarm

An electric bite alarm used in conjunction with a bobbin.

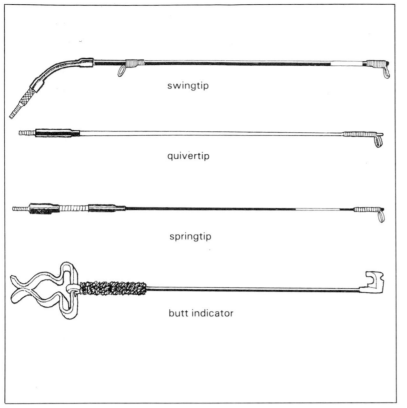

swingtip

quivertip

springtip

butt indicator

Four of the most popular types of bite indicator.

Opposite Fishing with a noticeable drift on the water. The angler at the rear is legering with a rod tip indicator.

you use the right weight bomb with the correct tip. Balance is extremely important otherwise you will not get fully effective bite indication.

In use, the rod is supported by two rests with the line passed through the ring on the end of the swingtip, which is then allowed to hang downwards. Swingtips are used widely on waters where the fish tend to be finicky. The rod should be positioned parallel to the bank or at an angle, depending on the terrain and personal preference based on experience.

Usually the strike is made when the swingtip straightens, although occasions arise when it is made whilst the tip is still moving upwards. Sometimes the tip will drop back from it original position; when this happens the fish is moving towards you.

Quivertips are used mainly in running water and consist of a length of very fine fibreglass, sometimes tapered, sometimes not. Like swingtips these are screwed into the tip of the rod. After the bait has been cast, the rod is placed in two rests and the current allowed to put a slight bend in the quiver. (Depending upon the current the quiver should either have a steeper taper, shorter length, or both.) When a fish picks up the bait the quiver will either pull round, straighten or pull forward although only a

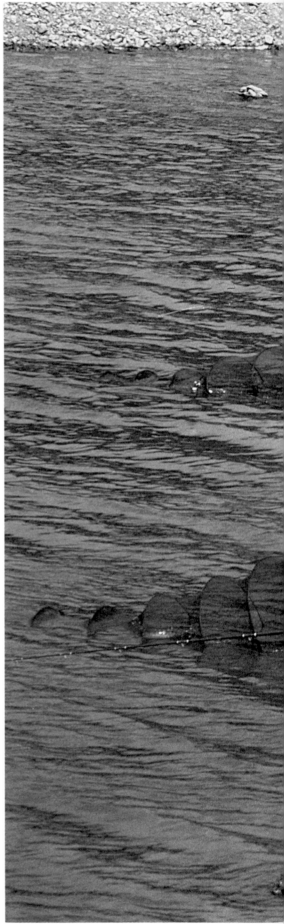

John Wilson netting an early season tench from a shallow lake. The fish was hooked at range using a swimfeeder rig baited with maggots. Note the fast taper rod which is most useful when striking at great distances.

little. Experience will tell you whether to strike or not. However, if it moves slowly, strike.

Because the top of a quivertip is so fine it is extremely sensitive and should at all times be fished with the rod supported by two rests.

A springtip is basically a quivertip with a light, sensitive spring between the base of the tip and the rod top. When a fish pulls, the spring collapses and the tip does likewise. Springtips are useful where the fish are particularly shy and might drop the bait when even the slightest resistance is felt. Immediately the tip collapses all resistance disappears.

Butt indicators operate on a similar principle to the swingtip, but as the name implies they are fixed on the rod butt by means of a Terry clip. On the end of the indicator is a ring through which the line passes. After the bait has been cast, the rod is placed on two rests and the indicator pulled down so it hangs at an angle of 45 degrees. One important point: the ring on the indicator *must* point upwards. Bites are determined by the indicator either lifting or falling back. Between the Terry clip and the indicator is a length of rubber which should be supple enough to let the indicator move freely.

When fishing with bobbins and butt indicators in stillwaters, the rod should be positioned so two or three inches of the rod tip is submerged; this way neither wind nor drift, nor a combination of both, will cause the bobbin or indicator to move, giving what is known as 'false bites'.

Baits and groundbaiting

Sometimes fish will take almost any bait you choose to use; at other times they can be exceedingly fastidious. A bait that works well on one water may not work on another; similarly a bait that works at a certain time of year or in certain water conditions may not work under different circumstances. In very popular waters the fish become shy of the commonly used baits — sometimes fleeing in panic at the sight or smell of a bait on which they have been previously caught.

For these reasons, amongst others, the consistently successful angler needs to know how to prepare and use a wide range of baits, the most useful of which are described here.

Maggots

Maggots are without any doubt the most popular bait of all. At one time shop-bought maggots varied in quality a great deal, but nowadays good quality bait is readily obtainable. It would be advisable, however, to go to a specialist tackle shop with a good turnover of bait, the sort of shop that offers a selection of maggots. Do not go to your local gardening shop that sells a few maggots as a sideline. Not only are you likely to end up with a lot of sawdust and comparatively few maggots, but in all probability they will have been kept refrigerated far longer than is good for them and will be stretched and tough.

Plain white maggots, fresh from the feed so they are plump and soft, are first choice. Some anglers prefer dyed maggots, even though there is no real hard evidence to suggest that coloured maggots are more attractive to fish, but anglers tend to follow the fashion in this respect. Maggots dyed with chrysodine, which turns them yellow-orange, once produced some good match-wins on one river and soon everyone was using 'chrysodines'. Anatto roll is used to dye maggots a buttery-yellow colour — these had a tremendous vogue a few years ago. Now the trend seems to be for bronze maggots. You can buy maggots already coloured, or for people who prefer to dye their own most specialist tackle shops sell the necessary dyes with instructions for their use.

You may come across very small maggots called pinkies. These are tiny, slightly pink in colour (hence the name) and used mainly for small, shy-biting fish in canal competitions. Squatts are also tiny; they are used mainly as feed because being much less active than standard maggots they are less inclined to bury themselves in the bottom, and can be incorporated into a groundbait ball without causing it to split.

Some match anglers breed their own maggots, maintaining that these are much more effective. The most popular home-bred maggot is the gozzer — a super-soft maggot used by bream anglers. If you want to try breeding them buy a medium-sized heart from your butcher, make two or three cuts through it, and place it on a bed of clean bran in a biscuit tin or similar container. Make a hole in the lid large enough for the fly to enter and place it in a dark, shady place. You should, if the weather is warm enough, soon get a cluster of eggs known as a 'blow' — probably in the main artery. The heart should then be wrapped loosely in newspaper and covered with bran to prevent smell. At the end of six or seven days you will have perfect gozzers ready to be riddled and placed in fresh bran.

For a short time after maggots have turned into chrysalids they sink — for this brief stage they are known as casters. They are superb bait and one of the best feed items of all — but home production is difficult and wasteful due to the critical timing required. It is better to buy these.

Bread

A piece of crust from a fresh white loaf may be pinched on the hook to produce a bait

that will sink slowly and rest lightly on weed or a soft mud bottom. Flake, as it is called, should be fluffy and jagged round the edges — it should not be moulded into a solid lump. If after a few minutes in the water it can be retrieved, then it has been pinched too hard.

A piece about the size of a thumbnail is about right for bream, tench, chub and big roach, although golf-ball sized chunks will be needed for carp. When offering small pieces of bread on a hook smaller than a size 14, many anglers prefer to use a bread-punch. This is a special tool that cuts and compresses tiny pellets from a slice of bread. It was popularized by anglers who fish for the shy-biting fish of shallow clear canals, but it can be effective for small roach in any still or slow-moving water where light float tackle is being used at close range.

Bread paste is made from the interior of a stale loaf (if you try to make paste from fresh bread it goes lumpy). The crumb is removed, placed in a clean cloth, wetted, and excess water is squeezed out. It is then kneaded into a smooth-textured paste. If it is considered to be too stiff a little more water may be added; if it is too wet, more crumb may be added. Some anglers maintain that paste should be very soft — almost runny, in fact, but very runny paste is extremely difficult to use. As a guide, paste should be firm enough to withstand casting and a gentle retrieve, but it should be soft enough to be readily dislodged by a false strike.

Paste may be flavoured and coloured by the addition of such things as custard powder, sugar, honey, soup powders, drink flavourings, and so on. It is debatable whether flavoured pastes are better.

Crust is probably the most potent bread bait, yet surprisingly few anglers use it. It can be used as a floating bait for carp, chub and rudd, an anchored bait which will rise as far off the bottom as the length of tail permits, or it may be used as a bottom bait which requires a little preparation at home. You need an uncut, close-textured square-tin or sandwich loaf, ideally two days old. The crusts are cut from the loaf with about half an inch of crumb attached, a pad of kitchen tissues is dampened and placed over the crust and a flat board with some heavy weights is placed on top. It is then left overnight. This treatment compresses the crumb, which causes the crust to lose its buoyancy, and also toughens it. Less damage is done to the crust if individual pieces of bait are cut rather than torn.

Worms

If there is such a thing as an all-round bait, then that bait is the worm. Although they can be bought from tackle shops and bait suppliers, it is cheaper and more convenient to collect and breed your own.

The most popular worm is probably the lobworm, the one that you can collect from lawns on still, damp nights. Unfortunately lobworms are not very easy to keep for any length of time, and they are difficult to

Some of these maggots have turned into 'casters' which make a superb bait.

51

breed successfully, so we are dependent on the rather erratic supplies that can be gathered after dark. They become very hard to find during a prolonged dry spell or a period of frosts. On a still, damp night they will emerge from their holes in hundreds, however, which is why the Americans call them 'nightcrawlers'. On those occasions they can be collected in vast quantities.

You need a torch and soft-soled shoes. It is best to wait until it has been dark for a couple of hours; the worms will then be lying out of their holes at full-stretch with only their tails remaining inside. Some anglers recommend that the worm is trapped with the fingers of one hand while a grip is taken with the other. A steady pull is then applied until the worm is withdrawn. Some inevitably break, and these should on no account be kept. Badly stretched worms will also soon die — and dead worms seem to sour and kill the rest. Lobworms are best kept in a mixture of soil, well-rotted compost, well-rotted straw and newspaper. This is kept in a bucket and provides a home for about 200 worms. They *must* be kept in a cool place — and it is important that an occasional check be made for dead ones, which should be removed.

To be on the safe side keep two worm-buckets on the go, then if disaster strikes one lot there is a good chance that the second batch will still be usable.

Redworms and brandlings are much easier to keep, and once you have obtained some breeding stock from well-established manure or compost heaps it is simple enough to start up your own wormery. Collect some of the manure and rotted straw in which the worms lived as a breeding medium. This mixture together with the worms is tipped into a plastic dustbin, in the base of which is cut an opening similar to the hatch on a coal-bunker — this permits easy access. The bin is topped up with grass-cuttings, kitchen waste such as vegetable peelings, tea-leaves, windfall apples, and so on.

Once you spot the clusters of tiny white worms you will know they have bred. The supply is self-regenerating providing you keep the container topped up with vegetable waste.

If you cannot find a source of supply for your initial stock you can buy a couple of tubs from a tackle dealer. With so few

worms you cannot expect rapid results and your wormery may take a year or so to become fully established.

Seed baits

The most commonly used seed baits are wheat, hemp, tares and sweetcorn. Sweetcorn may be bought ready for use in tins; the others require cooking. Wheat can be prepared overnight in a vacuum flask — you quarter-fill a flask with wheat, top it up with boiling water and leave it. In the morning the bait is perfectly cooked. Hemp should be boiled in a saucepan until a little white shoot appears. Tares can be boiled but tend to split, so a far better method is to casserole them. They are first given an overnight soak whereupon they

swell to about twice their size; they are then placed in a casserole dish, covered with water and placed on the top shelf of a pre-heated oven set at about 300°F (gas mark 3). After about an hour they should be done (a cooked tare can be flattened between thumb and forefinger). If they are not quite ready give them another ten minutes then allow them to cool naturally. Do not be tempted to speed up the cooling process by putting them in cold water as they will split.

Another good but neglected seed bait is malted barley. It is prepared in the same way as wheat.

Seed baits work best in warm weather — they are not very effective after the first autumn frosts. Sweetcorn is an exception

to this. A few years ago some astonishing catches were taken on it, but it appears to be less effective now. Too much sweetcorn went into our waters, drastically reducing its long-term effectiveness. An indictment of indiscriminate baiting.

Closely allied to seed baits are particle baits such as black-eyed beans, chickpeas, broad beans and red kidney beans. These have accounted for a lot of carp in recent years, as well as some good tench and bream. Broad beans and kidney beans can be bought ready-cooked in tins, but the others need to be cooked before use. An overnight soak followed by gentle simmering for 20 minutes is about right. Dyes and flavourings can be added at the cooking stage if required — chick-peas dyed red have worked very well on some waters, as have tomato soup flavoured black-eyes.

When these baits first came on the scene they achieved tremendous success — but this was short-lived, again over-baiting being largely to blame. A couple of handfuls are quite sufficient — and on no account should long-term pre-baiting campaigns be undertaken.

Special pastes

Prior to the development of high-protein baits, carp anglers devised a lot of so-called 'specials', most of which were meat-based. The two most effective meat baits were sausage meat and catfood paste. Both are prepared in the same way — the sausage meat or catfood is mixed with a cereal binder: this can be a proprietary groundbait, wheatflour or breadcrumb. It is then kneaded until a firm, smooth paste results. Meat or yeast extracts, soup powders, etc. may be added to give the bait extra flavour and to make it different to that used by other people.

But perhaps the best of the 'specials' is trout pellet paste. This is simple to make, although some anglers make extremely hard work of it by insisting on softening the pellets with boiling water or grinding them to a powder before mixing them with cereal. All you need to do is put a pound or so of pellets into a bowl, add just enough water to dampen them, then leave them to absorb moisture for half an hour. At the end of that time they can be kneaded into a nice smooth paste. If the paste is too stiff add a little more water — in the unlikely event of it being too soft work in a few more pellets and leave it to stand for a while, then knead again.

Practically every fish that swims will take these special pastes, although only carp anglers have really exploited them.

One of the most sophisticated bait developments in recent years has been the emergence of high-protein baits. Although mainly the province of carp anglers they are finding increasing popularity with tench and bream fishermen. At one time anglers had no choice but to make their own, and some were put off by the apparent complexity of the process. But nowadays you can buy various ready-mixes from specialist suppliers who advertise in the angling press. Dyes and flavourings are also available to add a touch of individuality.

To make these baits resistant to small-fry they may be mixed with beaten egg instead of water — if they are then boiled for about one and a half minutes they will acquire a protective skin.

High-protein baits are only really effective if used in conjunction with a pre-baiting programme. As a very rough guide fifty boiled bait-balls should be put in your chosen water twice a week for two weeks before you start using the bait.

Cheese

Although mainly associated with chub, cheese is a good all-round bait. It may be cut into cubes, or mixed with dried breadcrumbs and made into a paste. Any cheese can be used and a really strong Cheddar is popular.

Luncheon meat

This can also be used cubed or mixed into a paste. Although most makes are perfectly acceptable to the fish, the cheaper brands tend to have a rubbery texture which makes them just right for hookbait.

Fish

Loach, gudgeon, minnows, bleak, dace, roach, rudd, skimmer bream and small chub are quite commonly used as both live and deadbaits. But many anglers regard livebaiting as offensive so rarely do it. You will have to make up your own mind. However, if presented properly, the long term effectiveness of live and deadbaits is about equal. In the short-term it is perhaps another matter — there are days when livebaits are better than deadbaits and *vice versa*.

Sea fish also make good deadbaits, particularly herrings, mackerel and sprats. These have the added advantage that they are readily obtainable. It is not always necessary to use whole fish, incidentally, as half-baits sometimes work well, as do strips of skin with flesh attached.

Groundbaiting and swimfeeding

Terms change over the years. At one time 'groundbaiting' meant the introduction of any edible substance in the vicinity of the hookbait. Nowadays, instigated largely by matchmen, 'groundbait' means something much more precise: it is either fine crumb or a cereal-based mixture. The introduction of edible matter into the swim is termed 'feeding'.

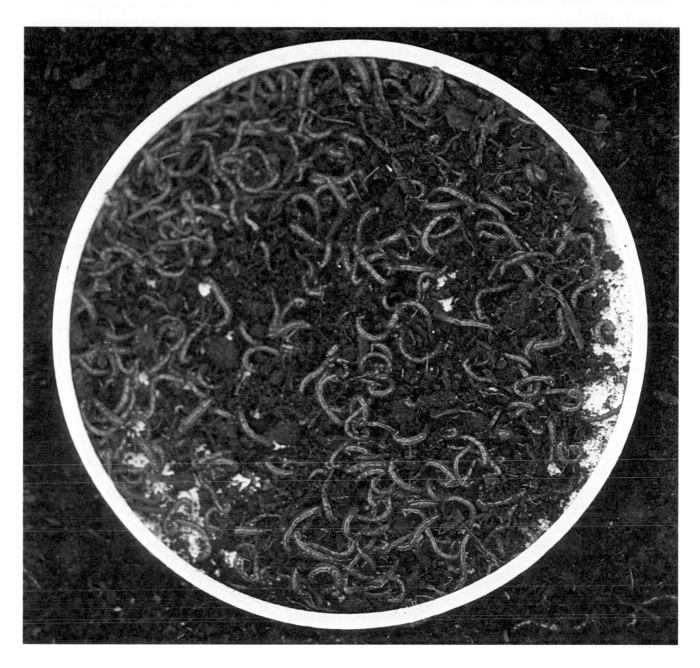

The most effective way of feeding a swim in most circumstances is by loose feeding. Normally the loose feed will consist of hookbait samples but sometimes it pays to feed with something entirely different, e.g. hempseed as feed and tare or caster on the hook.

Fine judgement is needed to gauge how much and how often feed should go in. Too little, and the interest of the fish may not be maintained. Too much, and you will satiate them. Ideally, feed should go in at a rate that keeps the fish actively searching for food. There are no hard and fast rules — half a dozen maggots with each cast might be plenty.

Usually feed should be introduced every cast — the hookbait thus appears to be a free sample. This approach should be modified if no bites are forthcoming, because there seems little point in feeding a swim in which there may be no fish. It is all a matter of judgement and every situation has to be assessed on its merits. We can only speculate about what is happening below the surface, which is why we sometimes get it wrong. There are times when you might fail to keep pace with the requirements of the fish and lose them. Conversely, on other occasions you might overdo it and kill the swim stone dead.

If loose feed cannot be thrown or catapulted the necessary distance on its own, it will be necessary to use groundbait. Although a number of proprietary groundbaits are available plain breadcrumb is as

A bait tin with a fine collection of bloodworms. These are, in fact, the larvae of gnats.

good as anything. White crumb makes a fairly solid ball that can be thrown or catapulted a long way. Brown crumb, on the other hand, makes a much more fragile ball. Clearly, therefore, you can exercise a fine degree of control over the break-up of your groundbait by mixing white and brown crumb together.

In still or slow-moving water it is usually best if the groundbait ball breaks up on hitting the surface, releasing a cascade of feed which will spread as it falls, thus carpeting the area. If it breaks up before it lands it will release a proportion of the feed too early and pockets of feed will fall all over the place — which may encourage the fish to spread too far. If the groundbait is too firm, solid balls of it will end up lying on the bottom. Although they will eventually disintegrate and release their contents, they will not produce the nice even scatter of feed that encourages fish to search an area for individual food items.

To mix groundbait you require a fairly large bowl — not a bucket. Put some water in the bowl and add the groundbait a little at a time, stirring and mixing all the while. Make sure that the crumb is evenly dampened. Every so often take a couple of handfuls and compress it into a ball until you are satisfied that it is the correct consistency.

For normal use it should be neither solid or sloppy — rather, it should be nice and fluffy.

Normally either casters or squatts will be added as feed, although virtually any hookbaits can be used. How much feed you incorporate depends largely on what sort of range you are trying to achieve. The more feed you add, the more readily will your groundbait balls break up. For long-distance catapult work you may have to halve the amount you would use for normal throwing range.

What size balls to use depends on circumstances — cricket ball size can be hand thrown quite well, but something far smaller will have to be used if you need to resort to a catapult.

As you can see, feeding a swim requires fine judgement, experience and finely developed physical skills. Anyone who has seen a man catapult balls of caster-laced groundbait 30 or 40 yards to the same tight area all day long can have no doubt as to the importance of the last attribute.

Good feeding is vital to success. Whatever your chosen field of angling, if you feed badly or are content to hurl out a few messy handfuls of stodge, you will never leave the ranks of the also-rans. But if you get it right you will be well on the way to success.

Opposite An angler about to load his catapult. Feeding a swim using a catapult enables you successfully to bait an area perhaps as much as 30 or 40 yards from the bank.

Bait Chart

Species	Favoured Baits
Barbel	Maggots, caster, worms, sweetcorn, luncheon meat, cheese, bread, special paste, hempseed; sometimes small livebaits such as minnows and loach.
Bream	Maggots, caster, worms, bread, sweetcorn, wheat, special pastes, luncheon meat.
Carp	High-protein pastes, special pastes, bread, floating crust, maggots, caster, worms, luncheon meat, cheese, particle baits.
Chub	Luncheon meat, cheese, maggots, caster, bread, floating crust, special pastes, sweetcorn, small live and deadbaits, crayfish, slugs, wasp grubs, artificial lures.
Dace	Maggots, caster, small worms, bread.
Eels	Worms, small deadbaits, maggots, cheese.
Perch	Small livebaits, worms, maggots, artificial lures.
Pike and Zander	Live and deadbaits, artificial lures, worms.
Roach	Maggots, caster, bread, worms, hempseed, wheat, barley, cheese, luncheon meat.
Rudd	Maggots, caster, bread, floating crust, worms, hempseed, wheat, barley, cheese, luncheon meat.
Tench	Worms, maggots, caster, wheat, sweetcorn, special pastes, high-protein pastes, luncheon meat.

Fishing for specific fish

Barbel

The first step to catching any fish is understanding its behaviour, and the lessons learned from one particular swim are a good example of this. The water above the small shoal of barbel was three feet deep, clear and every move that the fish made could be seen. On the far side of the swim was a large raft of tangled bush roots and accumulated debris. When they were not feeding, the barbel remained under the raft, secure and well hidden. Once they started to feed they moved out on to the adjoining gravel bar. On most occasions a feeding spell was heralded by numbers of fish 'flashing' on the bottom. As they became more agitated they turned over on to their side in a quick corkscrew motion and, for a second, there was a long gleam of ivory belly. Never did they perform this ritual without going on to take pieces of groundbait from the bottom.

The next observation is vital. Not once did these barbel take a bait that was not firmly on the river bed. Food in mid-water, or even an inch from the gravel, was totally ignored. The message clearly is that you must get your bait down.

These barbel approached baits in uniform fashion. They moved upstream to take them. They lay six inches away, watching for either a few seconds or, in isolated cases, for half an hour. Then, quickly and decisively they would glide up to the bait, their top lip would stretch over it and their gills would flare as they began to chew it. Sometimes with big baits there would be a few seconds while their barbules came over it, feeling and smelling.

No species of fish feeds constantly, but these barbel were almost completely susceptible to a lavish introduction of small baits sprinkled over the swim on the edge of the raft. Sometimes it would take merely a few minutes, at other times more than half an hour of steady feeding; but eventually the first fish would come out, give its characteristic twist and begin to pick the

morsels up. Once one was out the rest of the shoal would gradually show interest and appear.

Watching these fish for many weeks demonstrated that, unlike chub which swim haphazardly in the water, the barbel show great organization and keep to a strict routine. They simply moved upstream along the gravel bar, dropped back again in the current and repeated the process over again. They revealed great power — their big fins all came into play at once and their bodies torpedoed along the bottom with an almost eel-like motion. A big fish, once frightened, was all but unstoppable.

Certainly these fish were more willing to come out in overcast, damp weather but many fish were caught from this swim in blazing sunshine. Occasionally, if particles of food were well hidden in the gravel the barbel would root down to them, sending long thin streams of bubbles up to the surface. It was also noticed that the very biggest fish tended to be nomadic and rarely stayed for more than a day or two. But the smaller fish remained in the shoal for long periods. The barbel were not as easily scared as the chub were by the appearance of a human figure on the bank. It was as though their eyes were fixed very firmly on the bottom and what it could offer them. They were, however, remarkably quick to feel any vibration and their immediate reaction was to disappear under the raft again.

So how do you go about catching barbel from new and strange rivers? The first step is to find a swim with suitable snags. Barbel use these for both shelter and safety and it is rare to see them in open water for any length of time. Most commonly barbel lie beneath undercut banks, among the tangled roots of trees and bushes. They also like a raft of dead weed and river debris that darkens the water beneath. Often the fish seek out a snag that lies on the bottom, especially big sunken branches, or perhaps where small boulders form little caves. Of equal importance is the texture of the bottom. Barbel avoid soft silting areas and look for gravel, sand, chalk or firm mud upon which to rest. Weirs on all barbel rivers produce good fish, both in the whitewater and at the tail of the weir where the water runs fast and shallow; barbel are attracted by the food, oxygen and changing currents.

Barbel are one of the shyest fish and rarely show themselves, so it is important to choose the swim carefully. In some cases you can rely on at least some fish being present, but on ninety-nine per cent of occasions you have got to keep more alert for brief but dramatic glimpses of the fish.

If the swim is not too deep it is sometimes possible to see the fish roll on the

Weirs are especially good for barbel as they are attracted by the food, oxygen and changing currents.

bottom with a quick ivory gleam. This is a sure sign of a feeding fish, as are strings of bubbles, although barbel bubble more on some rivers than on others. The bubbles vary in size but come up in long thin strings. It is a fascinating sight to watch them slowly progressing upstream, and it is easy to imagine the fish foraging beneath.

Although barbel at one time or another will eat almost anything, there are two main types of bait. First is the large bait, the most important of which is luncheon meat. Generally lumps big enough to cover a size 6 hook should be used, although frequently in the daytime a smaller piece on a size 12 is best. It does not seem to matter if the meat is less than fresh for it is believed the barbel locate it by smell, often from some distance. Trout pellet paste has a really strong odour, and this can prove effective. Barbel also take minnows, cheese, lob-worms, slugs and crayfish but of all these big baits luncheon meat is probably the best.

The other type of bait is the small or particle bait. Introduced in large numbers, small baits totally preoccupy the barbel in a swim. They feed warily at first, but very quickly become greedy and lose all caution. As both hookbait and as ground-baits, maggots, casters and sweetcorn are of equal value. Fish two grains of sweet-

A fine barbel of 10 lb landed by John Bailey.

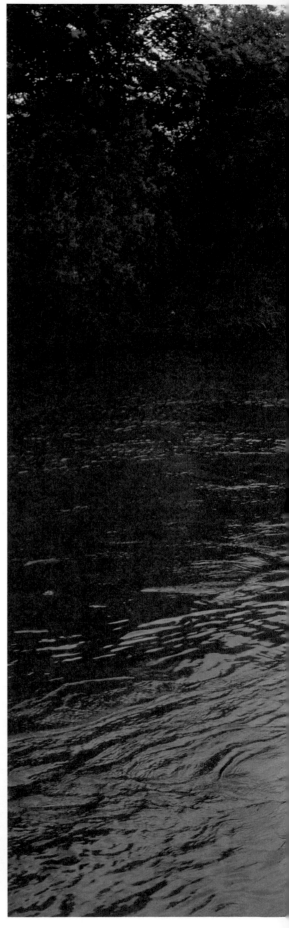

62

corn on a size 8, two casters on a size 14 or three maggots on a size 12. If the fish are very finicky then cut down the number of baits and the size of the hook.

It can take time to get the fish feeding on particles and sometimes a pint or more may have to be fed in, but if there are barbel there they will eventually begin to take. As a groundbait, hemp is especially useful. The tiny grains keep the barbel foraging long after they have picked up the more obvious pieces of sweetcorn. It is possible to overfeed barbel on hemp, and you should not put in more than one pint unless there are numbers of barbel in the swim.

It is absolutely vital to fish the bait, large or small, on the bottom, firmly anchored and stationary.

The easiest way to present a bait like this is to leger with a paternoster or a link leger rig, or even a bomb running on the line itself. It does not matter which, providing the lead holds the bait firm in the strongest current. In recent years the swimfeeder has acquired a tremendous reputation as a barbel catcher. When using maggots on the hook try a large size feederlink 8 inches from the hook. If using corn or casters pack a blockend feeder with hemp, as long as the current is strong enough to push the grains out over a five-minute cast.

For bite indication use a quivertip which is stiff enough to cope with casting heavy baits and for dealing with the strong current.

For night fishing you can permanently glue an isotope in place. A bite can show on the tip as anything from a series of tremors to a pull that takes it round two inches. Strike at anything positive.

Float fishing can also bring in good catches of barbel, but you must always be in perfect control, and it is not recommended to anybody other than those who are already very good at float fishing.

Match anglers are capable of playing out barbel on 1 lb line and size 20 hooks. They have proved that 7 lb fish can be landed — given time and space. On most barbel rivers, snags are too close for this gentle approach and the best advice is to go strong. If a barbel wants to get to his lair he is like the devil on the run. A typical barbel rig consists of a light carp rod, and 8 lb line straight through to forged hooks. Check for every possible weakness, for if you miss something the fish will find it — they are that strong.

If all else fails fish at night, where this is allowed. There is no doubt that barbel feed well after dark, and sometimes a dead swim can come alive after the sun has set. But make thorough preparations: fish the swim in the daytime and know where to cast and what snags to watch out for, and learn which pieces of bank need caution after dark. Take a torch big enough to bathe the swim in light if a fish is hooked. Remember that a barbel is a big fish which needs a lot of food and is likely to welcome your baits. It is not over-sophisticated, and once you have found a decent swim it is only a matter of time before one is hooked.

Bream

Bream are fish of still or sluggish water, favouring canals, lakes, meres, reservoirs and slow-moving rivers. They are sometimes found in the faster water of a river, but this is the exception rather than the rule. Of all the coarse fish, bream can be the most enigmatic and have, in the last decade or so, captured the imagination of match and pleasure anglers, and of specimen hunters too.

Catching any fish revolves entirely around the way we exploit their feeding habits. After all, anglers rely on the fish to feed on their hookbait, and to ensure that bait is presented to them in the right place, at the right time, and in the right way, we must first ask ourselves three questions about their feeding behaviour: where, when and how.

Where do bream feed? Whether we fish in lake, river or canal, we must first discover which particular areas the bream favour, because different species of fish are partial to different areas of a fishery; if we are not careful to choose the right spot we can at best catch another species, or at worst catch nothing at all.

The easiest way of all to find out where the bream areas or 'hot-spots' are, is to ask other anglers who fish the water regularly. If you approach the regular anglers and ask them where the best bream hot-spots can be found, most of them will be very glad to help you. They may not always tell you

A typical bream lake. Bream are a shoaling fish and often follow a fixed route through the water, which can sometimes be seen as they 'roll' on the surface.

where the best spots are, but it is certainly the easiest way to make a start. From this spot you can begin to fish and at the same time you can keep your eyes open and watch for bream — for 'spotting' is the second easiest way of locating them, and undoubtedly the most accurate.

This is because bream have a very obliging habit of displaying themselves at the surface. Bream anglers describe this habit as 'rolling'. What happens is that bream, being shoal fish, move along the bottom in a fairly compact unit, and when they are in a feeding mood a number of the fish swim up to the surface at regular intervals and 'roll' through it like porpoises. This rolling is what you must watch for when you are fishing. If you like, you can also watch for it during the close season when you are planning to fish the water.

Another of the bream's peculiarities is the way they follow certain routes through a water. When you have spotted them rolling a few times you will notice that the shoal follows the same track each time. This track may be a simple straight line, a gentle curve, a distinct 'L' shape, or any number of different patterns. The extent, both in width and length, will vary from one water to another according to the size of the shoal. Bear in mind, too, that there will probably be more than one shoal in a water, and the size of the shoals, as well as the size of individual fish, will also vary.

When do bream feed? This can also vary greatly from one water to another. A few waters are only worth fishing at night, for bream are perhaps more nocturnal than most other coarse fish. Some fisheries fish better in the morning, others are better in the evening. It is something you can only find out for yourself, either by fishing at all the likely times or, again, by finding an obliging soul who already possesses the knowledge.

It is important, however, that you do discover when the bream are more likely to feed on the water you have elected to fish. And a very good habit to cultivate is to make a note of the time on each occasion you either see the bream roll, or catch one. Bream are very clock-conscious, and after a reasonable amount of time on a water you will find that you can predict quite accurately at what different times they are likely to feed in different swims.

How do bream feed? The answer to that is related to their body shape. They are very deep-bodied fish, which means they have almost to 'stand on their heads' in order to take a bait from the bottom. It follows that a big bream will have to tilt its head through a greater distance than a small bream, and hence there is more movement when it straightens back to an even keel. This tilting is important and should be related to the amount of drop, or free movement, you allow on the bite indicator. The bigger the bream the more free line you allow them.

Some bream shoals, particularly those consisting of fish up to 4 lb or so, can be many hundreds strong. It is important to bear this in mind when groundbaiting. It is always difficult to know how much groundbait to take on a bream fishing expedition, for you never know how well they will feed. When they feed ravenously you cannot really take enough groundbait and loose feed. But on slow days it is just as easy to take too much.

The only answer is to get to know the water you are visiting and discover the average amount of feed you need for a day's fishing. Ideally you should always take enough to feed them on a good day, but not everyone will be able to afford that much, especially when the baits are maggots and casters which cannot be saved for too long a period. There are, however, a few waters where bread and worms are the best bait, and there you can take as much feed as you can carry.

A good groundbaiting tactic is to introduce several balls of groundbait, laced with hookbait samples, as soon as you arrive at the water. After that, it is a matter of feeding according to how well the bream are responding. Obviously if there have been no bites there is no point in introducing more bait, for we only risk overfeeding them if and when they do come on. The faster the bream are biting the more bait we can afford to put in, and with experience you will learn how much is right for different situations.

Other variables are the type of water you are fishing, and the size of the shoal. When canal fishing you may need to throw in only an odd handful of loose feed every 15 minutes or so to keep them interested. On a large river or lake several balls of groundbait laced with hookbait may be needed every few minutes. When the fish are very big and consequently very few in number, it may be better to throw in only an oc-

Graham Marsden with a large bream.

The head of a bream. Notice the underslung mouth, indicative of its bottom-feeding habits.

casional very small ball of bait so as not to disturb them.

Most bream fishing is done at quite long range, for on most lakes and meres the fish very rarely establish a feeding route close to the margins. It is only on canals and some rivers, or when boat fishing, that short lines can be used. For that reason, your chosen tackle must enable you to fish efficiently at a distance.

To begin with, the rod must be capable of casting weights up to about 1 oz and be equally capable of picking up a long line on the strike. A length of 11 feet is about right, with a test curve of $1-1\frac{1}{4}$ lb. It should be supple enough in the top section to cushion the shock of hooking and playing a good bream, but with sufficient stiffness in the butt section to cast and strike without feeling sloppy.

A fixed-spool reel is essential, with the line 3 lb breaking strain. A 4 lb line may be better until you have some experience of long-range fishing. Not that bream are tremendously hard fighters — but they do offer an almost solid resistance when first struck into, and until your reactions are

tuned to ease off as soon as this solidness is felt the strike is the moment when breakage is most likely to occur.

A range of Arlesey bombs from $\frac{1}{4}$ oz to 1 oz will be needed, with a $\frac{3}{4}$ oz bomb being the ideal weight for casting 40-50 yards, which is the average distance at which most bream feed. Always use the lightest lead possible after taking into account the distance you are fishing, the amount of pull on the water, and if there are any cross-winds.

For bread and worms use size 10 and 8 hooks. Maggots and casters demand smaller hooks ranging from a 12 to an 18, usually a 14. These can be eyed or spade-end, but the spade-end type tend to be finer in the wire and therefore more suitable for maggot and caster.

The paternoster rig is the best long-range end tackle. There are two types — one for fishing on or close to the bottom, and one suitable for fish which are feeding off-bottom or taking 'on the drop'. Only by experimenting with each rig, or being able to 'read' the bite indicator, will you know which rig is best on the day.

The most popular bite indicators are the swingtip and quivertip. But for night fishing an electric bite alarm used in conjunction with a glow-bobbin is better. The fish bite more freely at night.

The following is a description of what you might experience in a typical bream fishing session on a lake. On arrival at the water, in a swim you have already earmarked as being on the breams' feeding route, first of all catapult several small balls of groundbait laced with casters into the swim. Fire them into an imaginary circle about 5 yards in diameter; this is a small enough area to begin with, but not tight enough to make it too competitive if a big shoal of bream move into the swim.

Choose caster-laced groundbait, because casters are very good for holding bream in a swim for long periods. And as they are not a wriggly bait you can pack a lot of them into a ball of groundbait without fear of the ball breaking up in midflight.

Tackle up with an 11-foot rod, fixed-spool reel carrying 3-4 lb line, and tie it into a paternoster rig which has a 9-inch bomb length and a 3-foot hooklength. The hook is a 14 and the bomb $\frac{3}{4}$ oz, heavy enough to cast accurately to a 40-yard distant swim.

The indicator is a swingtip and for bait you might decide to try a bunch of four maggots.

Place the rod rest so that the rod lies at an angle of about 75 degrees to the bank. This will enable you to see bites comfortably and just give you enough of a sweep to hook the fish at the range you are fishing. After casting to the baited area, place the rod in the rest and carefully watch the swingtip, which is straightened out as the tackle falls through the water. When it hits bottom the tip falls back; tighten up so that the 12 inch tip hangs at 30 degrees to the rod tip. This gives the fish about 9 inches of slack to pull at, and 3 inches of slack to register a drop-back bite.

Within half an hour you may get the first bite. If you miss the first bite or two and find that the maggots have been sucked, change the 14 hook for a 16 with only 2 maggots. Perhaps on the next cast the swingtip does not fall slack when it should. Strike at once, and you may connect with a bream, that looks perhaps about 3 lb when you net it. You should catch several more bream from around $1\frac{1}{2}$ lb to 4 lb in the next hour or so, and then the bites may begin to fall off. Catapult in a few small balls of caster-laced groundbait,

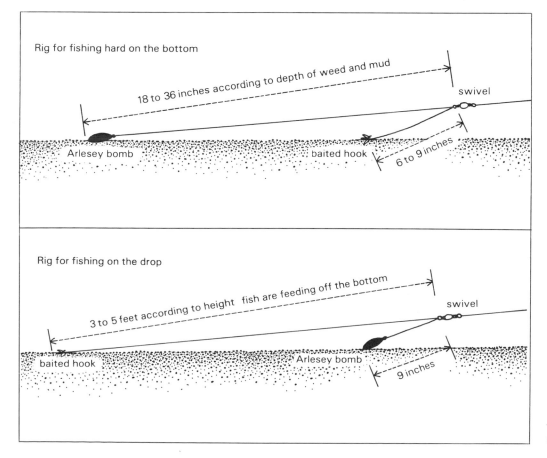

Two types of paternoster rig used in bream fishing.

An antenna float rig used
in bream fishing.

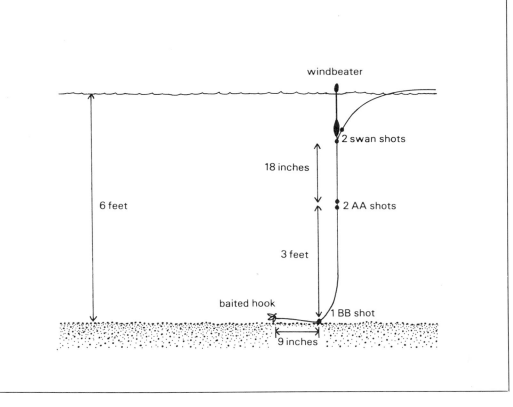

windbeater

6 feet

18 inches

2 swan shots

2 AA shots

3 feet

baited hook

1 BB shot

9 inches

mixed as soft as possible so that they break easily and with the minimum of disturbance when they hit the surface.

And that should be the pattern for the next five or six hours: feeding when the bites ease off; casting accurately to the baited area; carefully watching the swing-tip as the bomb hits bottom and the bait is slowly falling through the water; striking into fish with a firm, clean and controlled sweep of the rod, and playing the bream quickly but carefully to the landing net.

When fishing at relatively short range, such as on a canal or from a boat on a lake, you can float-fish, which has several advantages. The first is that a float rig allows you to use more permutations of bait presentation, from fishing hard on the bottom to using a very slowly sinking bait for bream that are taking high in the water. There is also less disturbance when a float hits the water, and the shorter range means we have no need to use groundbait at all, but simply loose-feed maggots or casters with a catapult.

Use a 13-foot match rod when float

fishing for bream, with an antenna-type float shotted as in the diagram. The bottom shot lies on the bottom and float will register a bite the moment that shot is disturbed.

Lines and hooks can be the same as for legering and the pattern of feeding is the same, except that it is better to loose-feed whenever possible (unless, of course, you are using bread as hookbait, which means you have to introduce groundbait to keep them feeding).

In canals, where the fish are generally much smaller and the casting distance is minimal (usually the centre channel is favoured by bream), the tackle should be stepped down accordingly. A short antenna float is still necessary if there is some pull on the water, but often you can easily use a short length of peacock quill or similar, attached bottom end only, waggler fashion. Lines need not be more than 2 lb breaking strain, and hooks of size 18 or even 20 are often large enough, for canal bream are most often caught on a single maggot or caster.

Carp

To catch carp regularly, it is first necessary to choose a water which contains plenty of them, and ones which are easy to catch. The beginner is well advised to ignore difficult big fish lakes which contain few carp; these can be fished later, once you have had experience of hooking, playing and landing plenty of smaller carp. Enquiries at local tackle shops, talking to club secretaries and visits to lakes and ponds marked on Ordnance Survey maps will soon produce information on likely places to fish. Choice of water is vital: many anglers have failed as carp anglers simply because they have chosen the nearest fishing venue to their home, without first making sure that there are plenty of carp in it.

Since carp are very much in the minority in most mixed fisheries, it is essential to spend the whole of each trip fishing solely for carp. The use of specialist tackle and methods will make it easier to sort out the carp from the other fish. Compound-taper through-action rods are suitable for most general carp fishing, but when fishing at

The head of a 27 lb carp. The mouth can extend telescopically for feeding on the lake bed.

distances of more than 70 yards or so fast-taper rods may be best. For open water fishing use 8 lb breaking strain lines, and for fishing in heavy weed or amongst snags, lines of 12 lb or even 15 lb breaking strain are recommended. When in doubt use a heavier line; the object is to land the fish – not to hook it and lose it, which is bad angling.

Most carp are caught with bottom baits. These can be fished freeline – that is, with nothing on the line except the hook and bait – or using legering techniques. When fishing at short range with a large heavy bait it is possible to freeline, but at greater ranges or with light bait you must leger.

A standard terminal rig might consist of an Arlesey bomb on a 3-4 inch link attached to a swivel. This is put on to the reel line, and a second swivel tied to the end of the line. On this is the hook link, which is 1 foot to 18 inches in length with a size 2 or 4 eyed hook. The swivel acts as a stop which cannot slip.

When fishing multiple baits such as sweetcorn, try a very light link leger with two or three swan shot.

Once you have cast out, the rod should

Jim Gibbinson makes some final adjustments to the bite indicators while carp fishing. He is using a combination of an electric alarm indicator and a simple plastic tube held down by a needle. The former will alert him to the bite and the movement of the plastic tube will show him more precisely how the bite is developing.

be placed in two rests, the front rest being of the kind which allows the line to run freely through the 'vee'. If you find that the carp in your water 'run' with the bait, taking line out very fast, the rod should be pointed at the bait to avoid the resistance caused by 'rod shake', and the bale arm of the reel should be left open with the anti-reverse on. When the line is being pulled fast from the spool, close the bale arm by turning the reel handle with one hand, almost simultaneously sweeping the rod back hard and high with the other hand.

If the fish 'twitch' at the bait, keep the

bale arm closed with the anti-reverse off. In this way, if you do happen to get a fast unexpected run, the reel handle will spin and your rod will not be pulled into the water. The rod can be parallel to the ground when fishing for 'twitchers' if you prefer this, but the strike should be made before the indicator touches the rod.

Missed takes are often a problem at first, so if you miss too many with the bale arm open try letting the line tighten after you have engaged the bale arm, only then picking up the rod and striking. Alternatively try the closed bale arm method. If you are missing twitchers try a longer 'drop' — the distance between the ground and the bite indicator — or open the bale arm and see what happens when the fish are allowed more line.

A simple plastic cylinder slipped over the line is fine as a bait indicator, and a Beta light (a radioactive light source) can be built in for night fishing. You will also need a 'needle' about two feet long made from an old fishing umbrella rib or length of welding rod. This is stuck into the ground pointing towards the butt ring of the rod and the indicator is pulled down over it until it is exactly underneath the reel to prevent water drag or wind from pulling the line from the spool when the bale arm is open. Many carp anglers use electric bite indicators, which are certainly useful for long sessions or at night. However, these should not be used without an indicator of some sort on the line as described. The 'buzzer' gives warning of a take, but the indicator shows exactly how the take develops. Use two or more rods where this is permitted, as you can then experiment with different baits and fish separate areas of the water.

Carp are powerful fish, so adjust the clutch on your reel so that line can just be taken from the spool by a hard pull — have it too tight and you will get a broken line; too loose and the fish may reach safety. Once the fish is hooked, keep the rod well up and play the fish using a steady strain, gaining line whenever you can. Avoid using the 'pumping' method, which involves lowering and raising the rod to gain line, as it tends to loosen the hook hold. If the carp bolts to one side for a snag, apply side strain by lowering the rod tip to water level and pulling against the fish with the rod parallel to the water.

Once the fish is beaten, lower the landing net — which should have not less than 36 inch span arms and a knotless mesh — into the water, and bring the fish over the net before lifting. Do not chase the fish with the net, or you may catch the line and break it. If the fish is large, grip the net handle near the netting with one hand, gather the mesh of the net with the other, and lift. In this way you take the weight off the net handle, which can break if subjected to too much strain.

Weigh the fish carefully in a weighing bag or sack and return it carefully to the water, supporting it upright until it swims away. If you wish to photograph your carp, hold it with wet hands as near as possible to the ground, and do not keep it out of the water for more than a few minutes. Never keep a carp in a keepnet, as these damage large fish.

Carp fishing is productive in many waters, particularly when the water is warm, and floating crust fishing is perhaps the easiest way for the beginner to catch carp. Fish freeline if possible, and grease the line to make it float. Cut a cube of crust from a new loaf, leaving a long 'tail' of flake to add weight. Compress this and insert the hook so it stands up on top of the crust. For longer distances, dip it quickly in the water and cast before the bait softens. If there is a wind, or much drift, use the anchored crust method. Most paste baits can be made into 'floaters' by adding eggs to the mix with some baking powder, and by cooking in the oven for about an hour.

Large paste baits can be cast very long distances when placed on a crust pad to prevent the bait from flying off. The crust pad is put on the bend of the hook and the paste moulded round it, with most of the weight resting on the crust. Modern baits such as pet food pastes, trout pellet paste and high-protein baits are very attractive to other species. Boiled baits mixed with eggs instead of water, and dipped in boiling water for a minute or so, may be needed to deter other fish. These can be mounted on the hook so that the point is exposed, making it easy to strike through the bait. Carp do not seem to take any notice of the exposed hook.

Some baits may attract carp very quickly, but when introducing a new bait to a water it is preferable to do some pre-baiting. This is best done twice or three times weekly for two to three weeks. Bait all over the water, with a concentration

where you intend to fish. The amount to put in varies according to the size of the water and the number of fish present, but as a guide 500 baits might be necessary in a three-acre water containing 200 carp. Boiled baits or those mixed with gelatine last longer in the water. For long-range baiting use a catapult, and do not bait up when others are fishing, or *you* may end up in the water! Before starting to fish, cast to the selected area and then put 6 or 7 baits round the baited hook. If you get a lot of takes throw a few more in when fishing.

Returning a fine mirror carp to the lake.

If possible try to find out what baits are being used on a water, which is often easier said than done, and what baits have been used in the past and are no longer effective.

Forget about night fishing until you are very confident with your daytime fishing methods, baits and landing techniques. Start your night fishing with short sessions, not by staying all night, and before it gets dark try to memorize landmarks and tree shapes on the skyline so that you know where to cast. Arrange all your tackle round you so that you can find anything you are likely to need without using lights — these may put carp off and will certainly upset many carp anglers who like to fish in the dark.

At first you may find it difficult to locate carp, so spend some time at your water looking for carp activity. Feeding fish may stir up mud and create bubbles; surface feeding fish will jump and swirl, and carp can often be seen basking on the surface, or cruising slowly with their backs out of the water. Watch weed beds very carefully

Playing a carp with a through-action carp rod. Carp are powerful fish and you should keep the rod well up and play the fish using a steady strain.

(using Polaroid sunglasses or binoculars): slight movements will show the presence of fish, and reeds will often jerk and 'curtsy' when carp are pushing their way through them. If no fish are visible look for shallow areas, sand or gravel bars, weed beds and snags, which are very often carp-holding areas, and try fishing near these. Overgrown and neglected areas where anglers rarely go are often carp hideouts. Walk very carefully when approaching such places, as the carp are often close to the banks — it is possible to stalk and catch large carp whose mouths are actually touching the water's edge. Surface-feeding carp make loud 'cloops' and these should never be ignored. See if you can stalk them, taking with you the barest minimum of tackle and baits. In rivers, carp are usually found in the still, deep areas such as weedy bays and backwaters, or in weir pools; in canals, weed and still locks are the places to look for.

Always carry several spools of line of different breaking strains and change over to heavier line before casting into heavy weed or snags. After landing a fish, especially in those snags, check the last few feet of line very carefully for fraying, and cut off any damaged line. Most breaks are the fault of the angler and not of the lines. Wind the line well up to the lip of the spool to make casting easier, and do not use one line for too long. Keep it away from direct sunlight as far as possible, as this may weaken nylon line.

Weigh your fish carefully and keep a record of catches, baits used, hours fished, and when fish are caught — it may help you next time.

Chub

The chub has large brassy scales and a huge mouth, with a correspondingly large appetite, and it is somewhat unpredictable in its habits. It is not afraid of tackle as a rule, and will take a big bait presented on a very thick line and a big hook; on the other hand it is afraid of human beings, and the angler who is not careful to avoid scaring them will not catch many chub.

In presenting these hints on how to catch chub it is worth remembering the useful formula laid down many years ago by Richard Walker for the consistent capture of good fish. The formula tells us that we must fish in the right place, at the right time, with the right tackle and the right bait, without frightening the fish.

Chub can be found in small rivers as well as large, and sometimes even in stillwaters.

On several major rivers there has been an explosion in the chub population in recent years. This is especially true of the Trent and its tributary the Derbyshire Derwent, where you can hardly fail to catch chub now. Other good rivers are the Thames, the Wye, the Severn, the Great Ouse, and the Yorkshire rivers Ouse, Ure, Swale, Nidd, Wharfe and Derwent.

For good numbers of medium-sized chub between 1 lb and 4 lb the middle and lower reaches of the big rivers are likely to be most productive. They seem to favour swims of medium pace, especially where there are overhanging trees and bushes. Willows, in particular, seem to attract chub, as do underwater snags, roots and weeds. However, if you hope to catch larger than average chub on these bigger

Angler netting a chub. These fish prefer medium-pace rivers with plenty of snags.

This young angler has caught a 4 lb 8 oz chub, which is showing its bronze scales to good effect.

rivers, you will need to locate the 'hot spots' where the large fish live. Often these are the most snaggy and inaccessible swims of all. Small rivers and tributaries require a different approach, as will be explained later.

So far as the right time is concerned, the chub is an obliging fish. It may feed at any time of the day or night, no matter what the season. But the peak feeding period is evening, starting just before dusk and continuing until about one hour after dark; the best months are from June to the end of September. This is not to say that there are not other favourable times. Dawn can also

be a profitable time to fish for chub, and in the autumn they are often willing to feed throughout the day. (Lobworms are a good bait for daytime feeding autumn chub.)

Sometimes chub are particularly easy to catch in mid-June, right at the beginning of the new season, but the fish are often in poor condition at this time and it may be better to leave them alone. If you do choose to fish early in the season then you can reasonably expect to find plenty of fish in faster, shallower runs.

For the right tackle it is probably better not to follow the example of match anglers

— they are obliged to fish at unfavourable times of the year, at midday, when conditions are bad and other anglers on the bank are frightening the fish. Therefore they often find it necessary to use small baits like maggots or casters, presented on the finest tackle, to be able to catch anything at all. This is rarely the most successful approach to normal pleasure angling for chub in more suitable conditions.

Many anglers love float fishing, but legering with a large swimfeeder like a 'feederlink' crammed with hookbait samples held in by a pinch of damp cereal groundbait is highly effective. All manner of baits can be fished this way, not only the normal matchman's maggots. Alternatively use a bomb or swan shots on either a fixed or a sliding link as terminal tackle.

Sometimes you can get fish on freeline tackle with nothing on the line except the baited hook, and this is the ideal method on small clear rivers.

A good line strength for chub is around 5 lb. This should be tied direct to eyed hooks in sizes 4, 6 or 8.

As far as the rod is concerned you will need a 10-11 foot model with a medium action similar to the famous Avon series. Swingtips or quivertips can be used but chub are bold biters and the rod tip should suffice. If necessary, feel for the bites touch-leger style, with the line looped over a finger.

Well-sharpened hooks and big landing nets are absolutely vital and artery forceps are ideal for removing hooks from the tough mouths of chub.

Chub will eat almost anything, but on most occasions it pays to offer them a big

Chub rising close to the bank. They have excellent vision and are easily alarmed so the angler must be cautious while fishing this species.

This hooked chub shows the large mouth of the species. Chub will take most types of bait, although cheese is often the most effective.

bait from the following selection: luncheon meat, sweetcorn, lobworms, bread paste, flake and crust, shrimps and cheese. The older and smellier the cheese is the better, as long as it is not so hard that it prevents efficient hooking. Cheese on its own is better than cheese paste mixed with bread. Processed cheese sold in square slices stays soft on the hook, even in cold water.

Do not scare chub. This really is important. Fish as far from other people as you can. Wear drab clothing — no white shirts or brightly coloured anoraks. Sit low down either in front of or behind cover, such as reeds and bushes. Sit still and avoid making vibrations. Too many anglers ignore this advice, which is one reason why many of them fail to catch good fish. It is even more important on small rivers.

Small rivers and tributaries that hold very big chub in clear water and snaggy conditions demand a special approach. Unfortunately many of the best of these waters have been ruined by pollution, overfishing and so on, but if you do find a

suitable place proceed as follows: begin by creeping and crawling into position so that you can actually see a big chub. Using strong tackle throw a freelined big bait as close as you can to the fish, and when you see him take the bait get straight down to it and get him out before his first powerful run enables him to get into weeds or snags and transfer the hook to them in some way. You get one chance only in each spot in a whole day. As a rule the best fish will be in the most inaccessible spots.

Although they are known mainly as river fish, chub do live and thrive in some still-waters, especially gravel pits where they often grow to very good sizes.

Pre-baiting definitely helps to gather chub in a swim. Choose a spot that chub already favour rather than trying to make them come to a spot they do not like. Put in plenty of lobworms, cheese balls, sweetcorn, luncheon meat and so on, for about ten days, throwing the bait upstream of the swim to allow for the effect of the current. This will give you a chance to get a really big net of chub.

Dace

Dace can be one of the hardest species to catch, and one of the easiest. Dace fishing can be frustrating — slight bobs of the float yielding nothing but a succession of shelled casters or stripped maggots. At other times, particularly in winter, they almost hang themselves, especially when there is extra water in and the level is dropping.

Dace have a habit of coming and going, and by casting a little farther out you can maintain contact when they seem to have vanished. And the fish that are a little farther out may be in the opposite side of the shoal, and have been unlucky in the scrambling rush for food.

In summer, dace occupy the fast shallows just outside rapids and some of the best catches have come from swims two or three feet deep. The floods of winter push them down into the steadier deeper water. Swim spotting is easy. The dace give their presence away by rising, even when the rivers may be coloured.

Not all dace rivers fish the same — they all have their own peculiarities. In some they are hard to catch, in others they are near impossible.

Tactically, fishing for dace is quite sophisticated. To deal first with the most up-to-date methods, which cover spate and hard to catch conditions, the roach pole has a part to play in big water when fish demand a slow or stopped bait. While conventional stick float tactics in slack water swims may account for 2-3 oz fish, the pole with a rig set up in traditional string-of-shot pattern will probably bring the average size to nearer 6 oz. But a word of warning — between summer and late autumn it is a devastating method for catching eels as well.

The float link — a method of float legering can be deadly in similar conditions. The set-up is simple. The float is a medium-sized balsa. Set up a link approximately 12-18 inches from the hook and on it place a couple of swan shot. Set the float overdepth and half cock so that the bites will cock the float and sail it away in one movement.

It can work with conventional rod and line, but it is a method better employed with a pole for greater reach towards the farther edge of a slack.

For a fish as canny as dace, legering might seem out of place. Far from it: a method has been developed using a butt indicator to catch dace in slacks. (In straight running water a quivertip would have to be used because the flow of water would lift the indicator to the rod.) The rig consists of a swan shot leger link with just enough lead to hold the bottom. This enables the angler to explore his pitch, starting on the edge of the flow. Every few seconds, ease the bait along gently with a half turn of the reel: the moving bait induces the dace to take.

Do not expect a sailaway bream-style bite. It will register as a tremor, a quick quarter-inch lift.

This method requires intense concentration and plenty of practice, and works to a distance of approximately four rod lengths. But master it and it can be a winner, especially in bad conditions.

Quivertips now come in varying degrees of softness, to aid bite indication. Again concentration is the key: you may have to rely on just one 'knock', and a quick one at that, to strike at. As with everything else practice makes perfect; but a good success rate would be hitting one bite in five.

Swimfeeders can be used to good effect in dace fishing. Some anglers have developed their own cone-shaped feeders, enough to hold a few maggots with a dab of groundbait as a plug. These can be made from discarded X-ray negatives if you can get them, otherwise waste 120 or 35 mm film will suffice. These feeders are rigged on the end of a leger link with swan shots inside and out, locking them on the line as well as providing casting weight.

Light tackle is generally best when float fishing for dace. The most favoured method is a stick float with a traditional string of shot ranging from the heaviest — usually a no. 4 — down to the lightest — either a dust (no. 8) or a micro (no. 10) — a foot from the hook. Choose an 18 fine or medium wire hook to a 1·7 lb hooklength. But if chub are likely to be present use a forged hook.

Any stick float range should cover both cane and balsa varieties up to 4BB, plus wire-stemmed sticks. The wire-stemmed floats ride turbulence superbly well because the stems are so thin.

There are times when a heavier approach is needed. This calls for a Pacemaker (a cross between a stick and a balsa, capable of taking a much bigger shot capacity than the stick). Balsas and wire-stemmed Avons also fit the bill.

And there are wagglers, of course, for use in downstream winds, which make floats attached top and bottom out of the question except for the highly skilled.

Casters are a good summer bait while maggots score well in winter. Remembering that dace can shell a caster in a split second, try double caster if you are having difficulty hitting bites, or when the dace are in a difficult-to-catch, float-bobbing only mood. If with two casters they still refuse to dip the float — this is usually when the river is low and stale and in need of an enlivening spate — switch to punched bread, feeding with soft breadcrumb groundbait. However, do not try bread if you have fed maggots. For some inexplicable reason the dace simply will not entertain it.

The following is a typical example of dace fishing in a practical situation. The time of year is October, when the river may well be carrying three feet of extra water. The river is coloured and the level falling — just the right conditions for a 30 lb catch. The swim is a slow to steady glide off the force of the main current, and about 6 feet deep. The wind is light and upstream, calling for a stick float. Tackle is a light 12 foot rod, basically tip action, but which has sufficient give to cope if, say, quality roach are encountered. The reel is a closed-face variety loaded with 2 lb line. The float is a 3BB wire-stemmed stick, with no. 4 shots strung out, the last two being a no. 6 and a telltale no. 8 or dust shot one foot from an

18 medium wire hook tied to a 1·7 lb line. Line should be soft and supple.

Plumb the depth, nipping a swan shot on to the hook, and set the tackle 8 inches overdepth. The idea is to slow up the bait on its downstream path, holding it back two or three times during its 20-yard swim down. This is so the bait rises above the river bed and falls when released in a manner calculated to attract free-feeding fish. Bait up with two maggots — if you hook

them through the nose or thin end, this will prevent them shrinking in cold water.

Everything is now ready to start. Feed eight maggots a rod length out and slightly downstream and cast the tackle so it descends with the loose grubs. Placing your forefinger on the spool of your reel, 'mend' the line so it is directly behind the float and start to ease it through the swim.

Feeding every cast or every other cast encourages a shoal of dace to move in. The first bite comes after the tackle has been checked, the bait allowed to rise and fall. The float dips away almost at the same time as the hookbait has hit the bottom.

If it is a good fish — between 8 and 10 oz — you may be met with temporary solid resistance. Do not try to drag it out of the swim: it may slip the hook. Let it have its own way for a second or two, then gently persuade it to move upstream using rod and reel synchronized together.

A typical dace swim on the Hampshire Avon.

The critical period is at the landing net. Do not let the fish flap on the surface. The hookhold may pull free, and the disturbance may scare the shoal. A few yards out ease it on to the surface, and with its mouth out of the water gently slide it towards the waiting landing net which will have been dipped into the water in advance.

When the fish begin to come steadily double the amount of loose-fed maggots.

If, as is sometimes said, the dace start 'crawling up the rod', you can comfortably change up to a 16 hook, sometimes a 14, to speed up the catching rate. There are times, however, when it is not so easy. You can fish that same swim with a similar set-up and water level without a bite, knowing full well that the fish are there. Step your tackle up to a 3AAA Pacemaker or balsa, stringing BBs out down to the last three shots which are a no. 8 a foot from the hook, a no. 6 and a no. 4. Set the rig 1-1½ feet overdepth and hold back hard. You

may then start catching. What may have happened is that a sudden influx of cold water has hit the river, and the fish require a bait either slowed up or slowed until it is practically stopped.

That is also the time when the pole tactics can be used to good effect. These tactics are confined to rivers which fish when there is extra water about. Not all waters do fish when the level is up.

In winter, when frost and sometimes snow are about, the position alters drastically. North country dace in these conditions are famous for appearing very late indeed. In the last couple of hours of daylight they start to feed. The first signs of fading light coincide with their desire to eat.

These hints are of course not the be-all and end-all of dace fishing. They are basic guidelines. Confidence is the key to good catches, and that confidence can be gained only by experience.

Eel

The eel is probably the most mysterious fish of all. Even today its life-cycle is not well documented. It is thought that only the female eel travels the great distance to the Sargasso Sea to spawn. From here the tiny eels known as elvers drift back on the Atlantic currents towards the coasts of Europe. It may take as long as three years for them to reach a length of only 3-4 inches as they drift on the currents of the ocean, before they start their run up river in spring.

They are very slow growing — an eel weighing 4 lb may be 12-18 years old. Today too many are being trapped by commercial fishermen in estuaries and rivers, especially in the Fens. They inhabit lakes, canals, streams, ponds, dykes, and so on — in fact most waterways. Undoubtedly the biggest come from the lakes and reservoirs. Small eels are mostly fished for. The big eels prefer a bottom of mud and clay.

One of the mysteries surrounding the eel is how it gets into pits and ponds not connected directly to any watercourse leading to the sea. It is clear that they must travel across land, and this is believed to happen on the darkest of nights, during a storm. The eels migrate back to the sea during October, and some very large catches can be made if you should be lucky enough to find them on the move. The largest eels never leave for the sea, but live out their lives in holes or among old pieces of junk that have been dumped in the water.

Contrary to popular belief, eels are clean fish, and baits need to be very fresh. Lobworms and small deadbaits such as dace, roach, bleak or gudgeon, or even fillets of fish are the best bait for eels. The only problem with worms is that they can easily be taken by the smaller eels as well as by other coarse fish.

Once you have decided where to fish and selected a swim, try groundbaiting with freshly chopped worm and fish. If possible, bait the swim each day for about three days before you fish.

Night fishing is undoubtedly the best way to go for large eels — the blacker the night the better. Dawn and dusk can also be busy times. (Obviously you should make sure that night fishing is allowed on your chosen water.)

There are no visible signs to show where the eels are, so the only way to locate them is by trying out different waters. Eels have a highly developed sense of smell, and it is believed that they will even venture out on to the bank at night to pick up surplus baits left there by anglers, but this is open to doubt.

Big eels will not venture far from their lairs and extracting a good eel from its haunt is not an easy task. It is an extremely powerful fish, and should one of them manage to get its tail wrapped around a snag it could prove almost impossible to move it. If you have this problem of a big eel going to ground, try the following method of moving him: keep the pressure on with the rod, then grasp the line between the first ring and reel and saw the line back and forth. This method sometimes works, although it cannot be guaranteed.

Warm dark nights are the best time. Start at dusk or at any time up to about three hours after. There will be a slack period until about 2 a.m. Bites then fall off again until just before dawn, when feeding can reach a frenzied pitch.

Take just the amount of tackle and equipment that you need at night. Have traces already made up. You will need a good sized landing net, with at least a $2\frac{1}{2}$ ft frame. A bright torch is absolutely essential, as it is no good landing an outsize eel in total darkness and then fumbling about for things.

Tackle should be stout. The rod can be the same as you might use for pike or carp — say 11-12 feet long. A reliable fixed-spool reel is essential, loaded with monofilament line of 12-15 lb breaking strain. You will need to use wire traces, for the eel has a powerful bite. Single-strand Alasticum wire is best, but avoid getting bad kinks in it. Stranded wire covered in plastic is to be avoided, for it has the bad habit of rusting invisibly inside the plastic.

Make the trace at least 18 inches long, and remember that a swivel is vital. Forged size 8 eyed hooks will serve for worm and deadbaits. A baiting needle is required for deadbaits: thread this in through the tail and out through the mouth, tie on the hook and then pull the shank back into the bait, leaving just the point of the hook protruding. The leger method is best here: slide a drilled bullet on to the reel line stopped by a split shot, and then tie on the trace. Lay the rod in two rests pointing towards the bait and wind up all the slack line. Release the bale arm and place a piece of silver paper between reel and first ring as a bite indicator. You can, of course, use an electric bite alarm, especially at night.

When the eel first picks up the bait it will take just a few coils of line. But wait — resist the urge to strike. It will then move off again slowly, then stop to turn the bait. It is at this point that the line will speed out from the reel as the eel tears away. Strike now, not viciously but positively: remember that from now on the objective is to get the eel on the bank as quickly as possible. Do not try to play the eel as you would any other coarse fish, for if you do you will surely lose it.

The eel uses its tail like a whip, thrashing furiously left and right. It can swim just as fast backwards as it can forwards, and should you let it have its own way it will most certainly find a snag. If you are fishing alone it is a good idea to have a damp sack to drop the eel into, cutting through the line above the swivel. After rebaiting and recasting you can get down to unhooking the eel.

Have plenty of rag around. Lay the rag out on the ground and then lay the eel on to it. Wrap the cloth around it, then, holding the fish behind the head, carefully extract the hook with a pair of artery forceps. Try not to harm the eel; put it into the keepnet if you want to retain it for weighing and photographs when it is daylight.

Remember that it takes a great many years for the eel to grow to large proportions, and with the pressures of modern society and the constant threat of pollution, the big eels are becoming scarce. Try to return all big specimens. A few

Opposite top Two types of eel fishing rig, both use a snap-link swivel.

Opposite bottom The angler displaying the eel that he was netting in the picture below.

Below An angler landing a sizeable eel. When you have struck an eel it is best to get it to the bank as quickly as possible.

smaller fish can be taken for the pot every now and then.

There is no doubt that the bigger the eel the smarter it is — they can even steal the fish bait clean off the hook. They have also been known to feed in mid-water.

A pleasant way of catching eels is to float fish around wharfs and rocks in estuaries and the tidal rivers. Let the worm bait trip the bottom very close in. The eels may not be of the large size that you find in fresh water, but good sport can be had with eels of 1-2 lb. Lobworm bait is best for this, fished under a perch float.

But if a British record-breaker is your target concentrate in any pit, lake or reservoir with a history of big eels. Perhaps the next record-breaking eel will be around 18 lb — it is certainly on the cards.

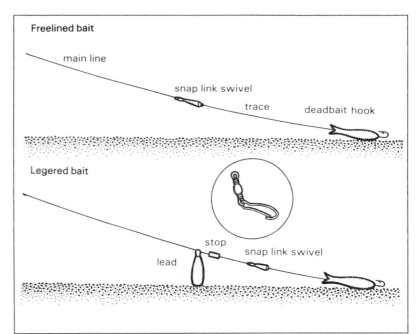

Perch

There is no mistaking a perch. It has between five and nine transverse bars along its flanks; the back is blue-green or grey-green, the belly silvery-white, the fins pink, orange or red. The back has a distinctive hump with double dorsal fins, the first being the largest and terminating in large spikes. The mouth is large, and so the baits do not need to be small.

The species coloration differs from water to water. For example, perch living in clear, well oxygenated water will have very sharp, bright colours, whereas those living in murky lakes will be much duller. They are shoal fish, and highly predatory. Their diet consists of freshwater shrimps, molluscs, small fish of every kind, worms and insects. The species is fairly evenly spread throughout Great Britain except perhaps in the far north. It is to be found in most rivers, canals, lakes, pits and village ponds, the bigger specimens generally coming from pits and lakes. They are prolific breeders and if food is in short supply they may become stunted.

To find the bigger fish, search out lakes formed from old gravel or brick workings.

To identify a spot in a lake or pit where you are likely to find perch, look for sunken trees or branches, drums, pipes or even old machinery, for it is in such places that perch wait for their prey. They do, of course, leave these areas when chasing their prey, as long as it is not going too fast for them to catch.

If you are fishing a river for this species, look out for eddies around bridge supports, areas of collapsed river bank, and so on. Keep a sharp eye open for telltale signs such as small fry leaping on the surface; you may also see small 'bow waves' appearing as the perch attack their prey. Lily pads and reed beds tend to hold minnows, shrimps and most of the other forms of life that perch feed on, so it is worth giving these spots a try.

Many anglers catch their first perch on maggot, whether by accident or by design, but using maggots can have drawbacks, such as small fish of other species pouncing on the bait before the perch find it. Pink or red maggots fished three or four to a size 10 hook are best — the perch seem to take pink or red maggots in mistake for worms.

Three types of rig for perch fishing.

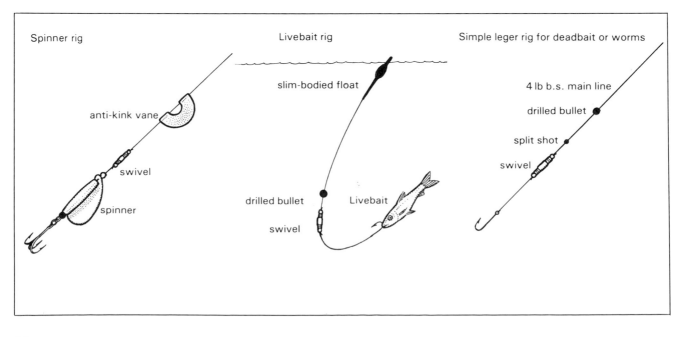

Spinner rig

anti-kink vane

swivel

spinner

Livebait rig

slim-bodied float

drilled bullet   Livebait

swivel

Simple leger rig for deadbait or worms

4 lb b.s. main line

drilled bullet

split shot

swivel

Brandlings, redworms and lobworms all take good perch. If you decide to concentrate on the bigger specimens you will need to get a supply of live and deadbaits (roach, bleak, gudgeon, rudd or dace) about 1-3 inches long. Remember to keep all baits very fresh.

Tackle for perch need not be too powerful. Any good float rod that you would normally use for roach will do for the average-size perch if you are using float fishing methods. There is no hard-and-fast rule for floats either. Any of the floats used for roach will suffice as long as it will suspend the bait properly without sinking, but do not overdo it by using pike floats. Use the smallest that you can, especially when livebaiting. In other words, if the suspended livebait can just about submerge the float on occasions then you will have the right set-up. If the float is too wide-bodied the resistance will not only tire the bait, but will almost certainly cost you some good perch when they reject the bait.

If you decide to go for the really big perch the rod will need to be more powerful. A rod of the Avon type, about 10-12 feet in length, will be about right. A good quality fixed-spool reel is essential, with a line retrieve ratio of about 4:1. A line of about 4-6 lb is as heavy as you need to go, whether you are float fishing, spinning or livebaiting — anything heavier is quite unnecessary.

A good guide to hook sizes is as follows: sizes 14-10 for maggots and worms, 10-8 for live and deadbait. Use a plummet to find the depth of water in the swim and adjust the float accordingly so that it sits in the water, allowing enough line — say 1-1½ feet — to lie on the bottom. You may need to adjust the depth to find out whether the perch are feeding deep, shallow or midwater.

In winter perch usually feed down deep, especially when it is very cold. It is at this time that perch frequent the deepest holes, patrolling up and down in search of food. Spinning can be very effective here.

The method with spinning is to fish slow and deep. Any hollow glass spinning rod, about 7-10 feet long, that is fairly powerful yet light and sensitive will be satisfactory; it should be capable of casting 1½-2½ oz. To set the tackle up simply tie a small swivel with a split ring attached directly on to the end of the reel line, then the spinner goes on. About 2 inches from the swivel attach an anti-kink vane — these are of perspex and simply clip on and off. This vane will stop the line twisting up.

There is little point in using a wire trace when fishing for perch — it only serves to impede the action of the lure. However, if pike are present in any numbers in the water, it is advisable to use a trace of single-strand Alasticum wire 18 inches long with 10 lb breaking strain.

The recommended method is to cast the spinner to the spot, let it sink to the bottom and then start to retrieve slowly. With every other turn of the reel lift the tip of the rod and then let the spinner drop back again — this helps to simulate the vibrations of a wounded fish trying to get to the surface. Also, alter the path of the retrieve from left to right, and back again. Never

Good specimens of perch can be found in large reedy lakes such as this. They can be difficult to locate, but look out for underwater snags such as sunken trees as it is in places such as these that they wait for their prey.

'pop' a spinner on the surface too soon: always retrieve right into the bank, for quite often a perch will follow and take the bait very close in. You can, of course, spin with worm in the same way.

Another method is to leger worm or deadbait. To make a leger set-up slide a small drilled bullet stopped by a split shot on to the reel line leaving a trace about 18 inches in length. If worm is the bait, use a size 10 single-barb hook. For deadbait use two size 10 treble hooks, placing one under the throat of the bait and the other in the vent. Set the rod in two rests with the tip pointing in the direction of the bait. Leave the bale arm off and attach a small loop of line under an elastic band on the rod butt in front of the reel (very lightly so that no resistance is felt by the fish).

For livebaiting select a slim-bodied float that is capable of just suspending the bait. Attach a small bullet or two swan shot to keep the bait down, then tie on a small swivel. Attach one size 10 or 12 treble hook, and secure the bait by passing one barb through the top lip only — this way the bait will be able to swim freely.

You will have to cast or lob the bait underarm, as any harsh treatment would undoubtedly result in the bait flying off. Let the bait work its way into all the likely looking spots. The sink and draw method can be extremely effective on the right day:

all you need to do is tie on a small treble hook and attach the deadbait by passing one barb through both bottom and top lips (in that order). Cast out, let the bait sink to the bottom, lift the rod smartly up and then let the bait sink back. Repeat this operation as you slowly retrieve.

A big perch puts up a good fight: it never gives up. You will feel the thumping as it tries to shed the hook. Remember to use the clutch on the reel — set it so that the fish can take line when it goes surging off, but not so fine that you cannot gain any line.

Try not to bully the fish; let it have some line at first, apply even pressure, and side strain should it be heading for a sunken snag. Once you have landed the fish handle it carefully. The best way to grasp it is to bring your hand down from the head, as this way you smooth down the dorsal fin. Be careful not to prick yourself on the gill covers, which have small protruding spikes.

Do not leave the fish on the bank for too long. Wet your hands and put him carefully back in the water to fight again another day.

September and October are the best months for the big perch. Like most other predatory fish they go on a feeding spree in the autumn to put on weight for the winter months ahead. March is also worth a try if the weather is mild.

Pike and Zander

Pike are not distributed evenly over a water; for some reason they collect in certain areas at different times, feed at specific intervals and show a tendency to be caught by one particular method.

Finding pike can sometimes be very easy. Any sudden change in underwater terrain, such as ledges and extensive weed beds, will be patrolled by hunting pike. The same is true of obstructions like sunken trees, fencing — in fact of anything that is dissimilar to the immediate surroundings. Valve towers and culverts on reservoirs, reedy bays, gullies and gravel bars on pits that meet in a central area will all be popular places. A straight Fenland drain that widens out into a bay on one side, or where a smaller drain joins, are also favoured points.

The most difficult positions to pinpoint are the areas known loosely as 'transient hotspots' — places that pike frequent in numbers for a limited period of a few days or weeks.

In the early part of the season, location of fry shoals can be of paramount importance. Pike will herd these shoals into enclosed areas and feed on them at their leisure. Alternatively, fry will be drawn to some spots such as warm shallows or where there is an influx or a drawing off of water, which in turn attracts the predator.

From January onwards female pike that are going to spawn early will group up in small numbers and move about with many male consorts in pursuit. Find these packs of roaming fish and half the battle is over. During the closing weeks of the season —

Andy Barker with a good size pike showing its typical torpedo-shaped body.

Andy Barker playing a pike to the landing net on a Scottish loch.

Some preferred methods of deadbait mounting.

especially if the weather has been unduly mild — many of these packs will integrate and settle for the same spawning sites. The angler will have a real birthday if he can find them.

Eleven foot, medium taper, lightweight rods of around $2\frac{1}{2}$ lb test curve have no equal. Use these with the old fixed-spool reels and you have a combination that cannot be surpassed for most forms of piking. Lines are a matter of personal choice — any line with a breaking strain of around 10-12 lb and which is reasonably soft and supple is ideal. Multi-stranded wire traces of 15-20 lb will cope with anything that swims. The current fashion is for Berkley Marlin steelstrand 18 lb test, which is best bought in 100 yard spools. Steer clear of plastic-coated trace wire because it is not very easy to tie, and the wire rusts once the plastic coating has been bitten through.

The majority of experienced pike anglers favour a two-hook rig using sizes 6 and 8

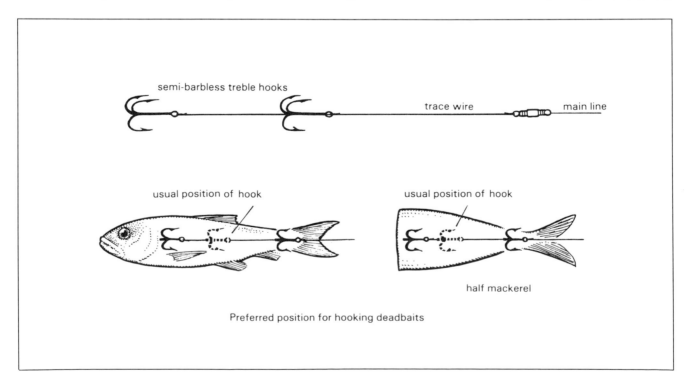

semi-barbless treble hooks

trace wire   main line

usual position of hook

usual position of hook

half mackerel

Preferred position for hooking deadbaits

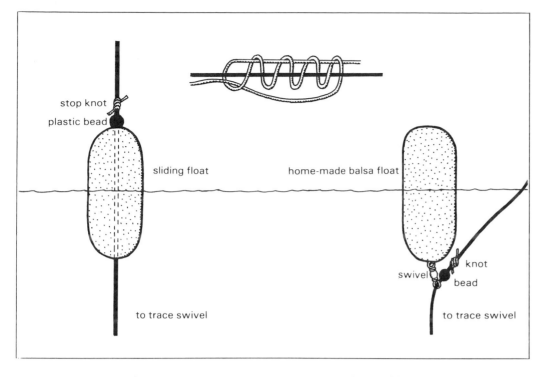

stop knot

plastic bead

sliding float

home-made balsa float

swivel

knot

bead

to trace swivel

to trace swivel

treble hooks, which will take most bait sizes.

To make a trace, cut an 18 inch length of trace wire, thread one end twice through the eye of a strong barrel swivel and twist the last inch around the main length, keeping the coils tightly together. Pass the other end of the trace through the eye of the first treble so that it slides freely on to the trace, and then attach the end treble in the same way as the swivel. With the uptrace hook sliding, different bait sizes can be accommodated. To lock the sliding hook in position, twist the trace wire around the shank three or four times.

It is not so much the *type* of hook rig that successfully catches pike, but the *placing* of the hooks. Multi-hook rigs are harder to strike home than two hooks in tandem. Many pike anglers, in their concern for not deep hooking the fish, place the uptrace hook in the tail root of the deadbait with the end hook two-thirds of the way up the side of the bait. The object of this is to keep the hooks away from the end the pike would presumably swallow first, that is, the head section (the middle in the case of half baits). Clearly, if the bait is grabbed and held in the area above the end hook, the resulting strike fails to drive the hooks home since they are outside the pike's mouth. Waiting for the fish to take a firmer hold on the bait could result in a deeply hooked fish. The only practical way both to strike early and to prevent deep hooking

is to place the end hook near the *front* of the bait. A pike picking up the bait by the tail or head section is in a position to be hooked by the treble hook fixed there. Should it be so bold as to take the bait round the middle, then the trace wire running between the hooks would be in its jaws. The strike would pull the end treble hook into the outside of its jaw — a ruse that has worked too many times for it to be pure luck.

The use of a small oilstone to hone the points of the hooks to razor sharpness, so that they easily penetrate the flesh, ensures that the fish do not drop off on the way into the net, even when hooked in the boniest regions of the jaws.

The most significant development in pike and zander fishing in recent years has been the extensive use of 'semi-barbless trebles' by many experienced anglers. Tests have shown that although shop-bought treble hooks are adequate, the barbs are usually too rank and prevent the hook sliding home up to the bend ensuring a good hold. One rank barb only should be left to impale the bait — the other two barbs should be squeezed back against the main wire from which they were cut. This leaves two slight bumps which provide less resistance on the strike. Penetration is increased, and the compressed barbs still offer enough resistance to stop the hook dropping out should a mishap occur during the playing of the fish.

Unhooking procedures have also developed in recent years. The 'gagless' method involves gripping the lower jaw by sliding the fingers of one hand into the mouth via the gill aperture, and holding the flesh tight between the fingers and palm of the hand. A pair of forceps is then wriggled between the jaws to prise them open if the fish proves unco-operative. *But this method should only be practised by the experienced angler*, otherwise slashed fingers might result. A better method is to use a medium-sized gag with the points masked by tape to stop them ripping the flesh. Place it in the centre of the mouth and not to the side, otherwise the fish can spit it out.

For the lone angler, unhooking a lively fish can be a big problem. The solution is to straddle the fish, kneeling over it with one leg either side, and facing its head. The fish sits on its stomach in the grass, and if it tries to thrash about then gentle pressure exerted on it by the legs will quell any movement. Lean forward and, with the gag in place, you can hold the trace wire taut in one hand; using a pair of 8 inch artery forceps in the other, you can quite easily deal with any hooks positioned near the front of the mouth.

The difficulty arises when the hooks are well back, by or in the throat tissue. The best way to deal with these is by getting the forceps into the mouth via the gill rakers. Make sure that the forceps are closed on entry, otherwise they may rip the very fragile filaments on the gill rakers, causing extensive bleeding. It is often necessary to use a second pair of forceps the same size as the first. The trick is to clamp the jaws of the first pair around the shank of the treble hook and twist it so that the points of the hook point towards the tail: with them held in this position the second pair of forceps is brought in via the gill raker opening on the other side and gently closed around the flesh on the hook. The flesh can then be lifted off the rank barb, whereupon it will slide off the bumps of the other two points.

When a hook is well and truly lodged in the stomach and will not come into view, even when gentle pressure has been applied by pulling on the trace wire, it is best left in the fish. Cut the trace as near to the hook as possible with a small pair of wire cutters.

After unhooking weigh the fish in a large plastic bag or a micromesh knotless type net. Make sure that the net is wet before placing the fish in it, so as to remove as little slime and scales from the fish as possible. Normally fish should be returned immediately, but sometimes it is nice to get a good bag of fish and photograph them together at the end of the day. But do not overcrowd the keepnet, otherwise the fish may suffer.

Bale arms on reels are always left open at any time when the rod is not being held,

A 22 lb pike showing its rows of sharp teeth.

A fine haul of two zander and two pike.

otherwise a fish could take the bait and then eject it because the line cannot be drawn freely from the spool.

Loop an elastic band around the rod handle just above the reel fitting to tuck a loop of line under when the bale arm is left open. This is a good idea, especially on windy days, as it stops the line being blown off in coils around the reel handle and rod rest. When the bait is taken, the loop of line is pulled out of the elastic band and runs freely from the spool.

The pike angler's greatest moment surely comes at about eleven o'clock in the morning when, as the last vestiges of frost melt away in the rising sun, a big female pike lifts herself lazily off the bottom and catches sight of a float-fished paternostered livebait in front of her. On the surface the float bobs and then slides away as she takes the bait. A quick movement and the angler is by the rod; the line now trickles steadily off the spool, having pulled out from the elastic band.

The fish bores off, out from the bank. The clutch must be locked up tight so that it cannot slip, with the anti-reverse off so that you can play the fish from the reel handle by backwinding to give her line if she proves lively. This is a far more satisfactory method than using an unreliable (in most cases) clutch mechanism.

Quickly wind in the slack line, slowly swinging the tip of the rod round to point at the position where the fish is running to. The line tightens from rod tip to running fish. Then, as you feel weight and resistance on the winding reel handle, raise the rod to a near vertical position and pull the hooks into her jaw on the strike. Giving her no slack line, wind down again and pull back on her ponderous weight, then start pumping her in. Perhaps she kites to the left: lay the rod over to the right and she

Landing a zander from a typical stretch of lowland water.

comes back on course. She will thrash and shake her head in defiance, but keep calm as you play her out. Kneel down and reach out for your landing net, which you have laid by your side at the start of the run; slide it into the water in front of you. The middle finger of your right hand touches the spool to stop the reel giving line. The great pike finally gives up and lies there in front of you as you pull back on the rod. Over the mouth of the net she slides, and she is yours.

Zander fishing is really nothing more than a modified form of pike fishing.

Zander will not tolerate resistance — large floats and big treble hooks. When

The head of a young zander showing its teeth.

feeding ravenously they will tackle anything, but more often than not they are finicky feeders. Whereas pike will kill and eat in the same action, zander will attack bait fish, maim or kill several, and then come back later to clean them up.

It is very easy to tell when a zander has mouthed the bait and then ejected it, because their teeth are shorter and stubbier than a pike's and they leave nailpunch-like holes in the bait, sometimes in a 'vee' pattern.

Zander behaviour is fairly predictable. They tend to hunt in packs of perhaps a dozen fish, although there may sometimes be up to forty or more. Therefore, when a pack has been located many fish may be caught before they move on.

The months from August and September onwards are when they are at their best, feeding well at dawn and dusk, sometimes until well after dark on warm and overcast nights. They intensely dislike very cold conditions, when there is a lot of snow and ice around, and will not feed.

Very often they will feed avidly in hot sunny conditions for no apparent reason, and on some small drains will dash out and attack a bait presented right up against the lily pads and reed beds they are hiding in.

Except for a few spots on certain drains that consistently produce zander, location is rather a hit-and-miss affair. The best way is to find the bait fish first, and zander will not be far away.

When float fishing for pike and zander use a sliding float — either the plastic celluloid type in which the line passes through the middle, or a home-made balsa type about 4 inches long which slides up and down via a link swivel. The link means that the float can be changed for one of a different size or colour at a moment's notice.

A Billy Lane sliding stop-knot is tied to the reel line in the required position. Then a small bead is threaded on, followed by the float. The bead is necessary to arrest the float against the stop-knot, because some shop-bought floats, having a bigger bore

A fine zander showing the spiky dorsal fin typical of members of the perch family.

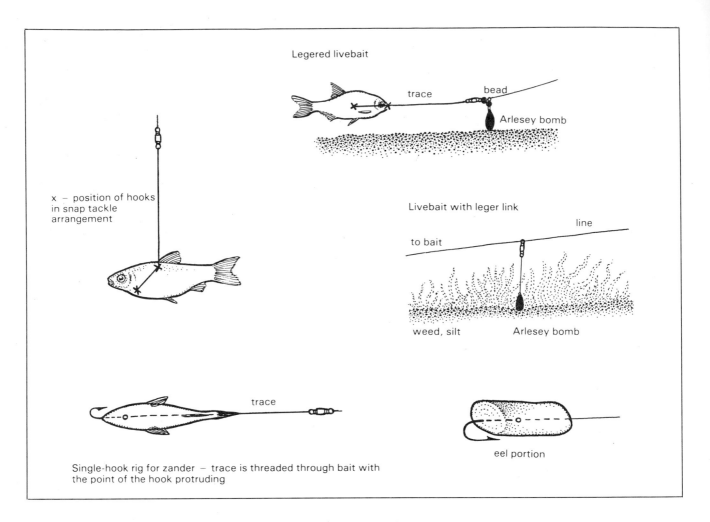

Legered livebait

trace

bead

Arlesey bomb

x – position of hooks in snap tackle arrangement

Livebait with leger link

line

to bait

weed, silt

Arlesey bomb

trace

eel portion

Single-hook rig for zander – trace is threaded through bait with the point of the hook protruding

Some different rigs for pike and zander fishing.

than the diameter of the knot, would otherwise slide over it. The trace wire is tied on and swan shot gently nipped on to the line above the trace to cock the float. To alter the depth, slightly moisten the sliding knot and slide it along the main line to the required position.

Perhaps the most deadly of all livebait methods, and one that has taken many big zander and pike, is the float paternoster rig. This is made simply by the addition of an Arlesey bomb of $\frac{1}{2}$-1 oz (depending on conditions such as water flow, wind, etc.) to the usual float set-up. The Arlesey bomb is joined to the trace swivel by a length of fine line of about 5 lb breaking strain. This anchors the livebait in one position, whereupon it will make repeated attempts to get away. The vibrations it gives off are irresistible to the predatory fish in the vicinity.

On some days when other anglers' baits remain untouched this method will take fish after fish. The length of the weak line, or 'rotten bottom' as it is called (the purpose of which is to enable the lead to break free in the event of it becoming snagged

during the playing of the fish) depends on how far off the bottom the bait is to be fished. Some anglers prefer to tie the link halfway down the trace to keep the livebait working deep. Occasionally some livebaits, such as rudd, swim up and tangle the trace wire around the swan shot on the line. To prevent this, always position the lead further up the line than the length of the trace.

When livebaiting for pike and hoping for zander as well, the hook size is determined by the size of the bait. For instance, on a 6 oz livebait use two size 8 treble hooks which will cope with both species. Zander attack biggish livebaits with a gusto that has to be seen to be believed, and they do not seem to be put off by the size of the ironmongery present.

On wide waters, livebaits can be legered for zander and pike at long distances. To do this remove the swan shot, float and sliding knot from the line and slide on a 1-2 oz Arlesey bomb using a link swivel to the lead. A plastic bead holds the link swivel off the main line knot to trace swivel, so that no undue stress is put on the knot during casting. Normally, float-fished livebaits are hooked up using the standard snap tackle arrangement: end hook nicked into the muscle of the pectoral fin and uptrace hook implanted firmly into the muscle of the dorsal fin. This is the oldest and most popular hooking rig in use, but if employed on legered livebaits would make them keel over and lie on their sides. A better arrangement is to hook the bait through the lips with the uptrace hook and place the end hook in the dorsal fin muscle. This will ensure that the livebait can work freely.

The same tackle assembly can be used with both freshwater and sea fish deadbaits for pike, although perhaps a running link leger would be better on weedy or muddy bottoms. Deadbaits are hooked on near the head and tail as described earlier. With sprats, being a soft bait, the uptrace hook is positioned through both eyes as this is the strongest hold available.

Large deadbaits such as mackerel and herring are usually freelined, because they are heavy enough not to need lead on the line to achieve the required distance. Half baits are often used, the tail portions of mackerel, herring and big freshwater baits being the commonest.

It is rare to catch zander on seafood baits — they are just not interested in them. Freshwater deadbaits are a different story, and so is bait presentation. Small treble hooks (10-14) are used to cut down the number of dropped runs that occur with deadbaiting. In the case of really finicky zander a large single hook is used, the trace

A float paternoster rig with a live bait (below) and two methods of bite indication (left and bottom).

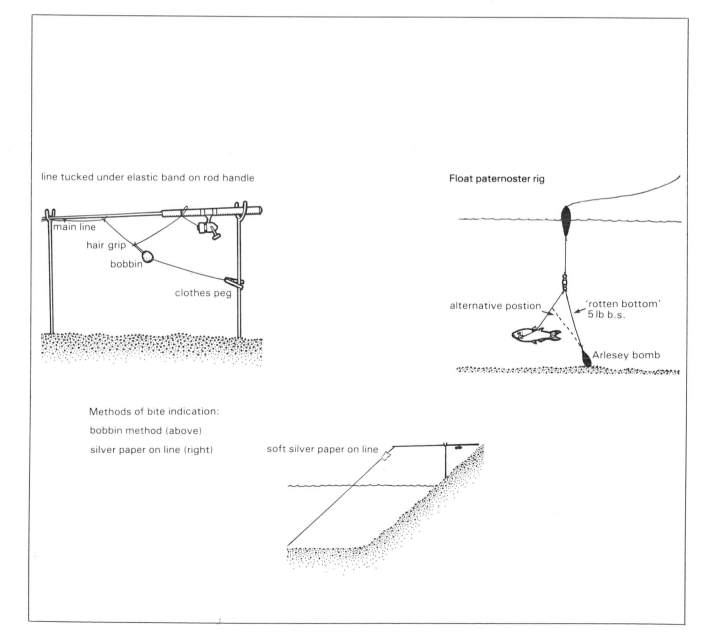

line tucked under elastic band on rod handle

main line

hair grip

bobbin

clothes peg

Methods of bite indication:
bobbin method (above)
silver paper on line (right)

Float paternoster rig

alternative postion

'rotten bottom' 5 lb b.s.

Arlesey bomb

soft silver paper on line

being threaded through the body of the bait with a baiting needle leaving just the point and barb showing. This way the zander will not feel any metal until it turns the bait ready to swallow — zander are peculiar in that they always swallow tail first; pike virtually always take the prey head first.

Recently some anglers have been experimenting with small portions of eel for bait, threaded on to a 1 or 2 O hook with trace, and results have been excellent with many big fish coming to the net.

Bite indication for legered and freelined baits is very simple. With the rod in the rests, the bale arm is left open and a cylinder of aluminium foil or silver paper placed on the line between the reel spool and butt ring. The drawback with silver paper or plastic rings is that they have to be left on during the playing of the fish or removed during the initial run. The most popular alternative is a kind of bobbin, which can be made at home from a table-tennis ball, or a piece of balsa wood, painted fluorescent orange and with a hair grip or similar clip attached. This clip is attached to the line. Fixed to the back of the bobbin is a fine piece of cord, the other end of which is fixed to a clothes peg. The clothes peg in turn clamps on to the back rod rest. When a fish takes the bait the line is pulled out of the hair grip, whereupon the bobbin falls to the ground, signalling a run. When using freelined baits it is advisable to make sure that the bobbin is heavy enough to drop down to signal a slack line bite if the fish swims towards the angler with the bait. Another method, and one favoured by zander anglers when fishing waters that have high banks, is to tuck the line under an elastic band on the rod handle as described above, and to squeeze a small piece of soft silver paper on to the line below the rod tip. A take will be indicated by the silver paper moving down towards the water as the fish takes the line.

If zander are caught by twitching and wobbling deadbaits or by plugging and spinning, it is probably more by accident than design. This is mainly because no one has seriously tried to adapt these methods for zander.

For pike on the other hand, twitching and wobbling deadbaits can prove highly effective at times. (The term 'twitching' usually means slowly inching a deadbait back across the bottom, although it also works with other baits and the speed of retrieve can be varied.)

For wobbling mount a bait on the standard two-hook rig, perhaps with lead on the trace or line, in such a way that a certain action that incites pike to attack will be imparted to it as it is retrieved. The uptrace hook is placed through the lower jaw and out through the skull — giving a very strong hold for casting. A swan shot on the trace helps to impart the desired action.

For plugging and spinning you will need a short trace of about 12 inches with a link swivel at the end to ensure speedy interchangeability of lures.

There are many successful plugs, spoons and spinners on the market, and it is really up to each individual angler to find out by experience which one suits him best.

Roach

Roach are the most widely distributed of our coarse fish species and are found everywhere from tiny overgrown streams and village ponds to the rich, fast flowing rivers, lakes, gravel pits and huge reservoirs. They are prolific breeders, and so become very much a shoal fish, sometimes with as many as several hundred living as a single unit within the boundaries of their home or swim.

When frightened the shoal will stop feeding, and in some cases it might even vacate the swim. So treat the roach with caution. Be careful in your approach and handle the fish delicately, whether hook-ing or unhooking and returning. The layer of mucus covering the scales acts as a protection against parasites, and it will be easily rubbed off by the angler who does not wet his hands before holding his catch, leaving the roach vulnerable to disease.

Roach are also delicate in the way they feed. Compare the mouth of a six-inch roach to that of a similar sized chub, bream or carp, and you will see that vast quan-tities of food are not consumed at one time as they are in the case of bream, for in-stance. The old adage concerning roach fishing — feeding them little and often — could not be more true, particularly when

A catch of river roach in superb condition taken on leger tackle in late autumn.

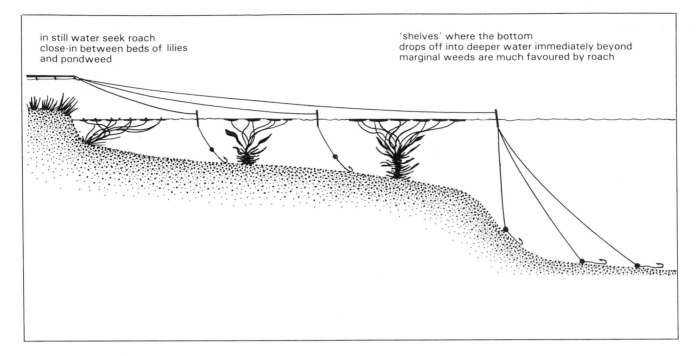

in still water seek roach
close-in between beds of lilies
and pondweed

'shelves' where the bottom
drops off into deeper water immediately beyond
marginal weeds are much favoured by roach

Suitable spots to fish for
roach in ponds and lakes.

Opposite A specimen
roach. These fish are easily
damaged so it is important
to handle them carefully.

larger specimens weighing a pound or more, which are invariably found in small shoals, are caught. There is no point in throwing in several handfuls of maggots before your first cast if only a dozen roach actually live in the swim you have chosen. You would overfeed them before even getting a bite, and probably either conclude that the swim was barren or that its occupants were off the feed. The first lesson on roach fishing, therefore, is to imagine the size of shoal in front of you, and to feed accordingly.

For optimum control and for hitting those shy bites, a 13 foot rod with a light, yet crisp action will be found ideal for all float fishing. You could use the same rod for legering at a pinch — if the tip ring has a screw thread to take either a swingtip or quivertip. A second, shorter, legering rod is, however, advisable and nicer to use. A length of between 9 and 11 feet is ideal, and again a screw-in tip ring is recommended.

Reel choice can be either a fixed-spool, closed face or a centre-pin. A fixed-spool is usually preferred for legering or for float fishing more than 3 rod lengths out, and a free flowing centre-pin for more delicate control when float fishing close in. But overall, a lightweight fixed-spool reel loaded with 2 lb breaking strain line for float work and a spare spool containing 3 lb line for legering should cover all eventualities. In addition to a selection of floats and leger bombs, your kit should also con-

tain some small size 14-20 hooks tied to 1½ lb breaking strain line for a more natural presentation of small baits such as maggots, and of course eyed hooks from size 12 to size 8 for offering large bread or worm baits. Always tie larger hooks direct to the reel line.

The secret of success in stillwater roaching is never to fish further out than you need to, because float control becomes more difficult, especially in strong winds. Legering is the alternative, otherwise there are special techniques for long-range float fishing which will be dealt with later. But to begin with seek roach close in: they often actually prefer to inhabit swims along the margins, for the richer grazing and natural food that warmer shallow water provides. Clear areas in shallow lakes between large beds of floating weeds such as broadleaved potamogeton or lilies are usually worth a try, because they provide both food and cover. So too are 'shelves' where the bottom drops off into deeper water immediately beyond the marginal beds. If these natural holding areas cannot be seen then plummet carefully up to two rod lengths out to get an idea of the bottom topography before choosing a swim.

Select a light float (a porcupine or peacock quill holding 2BB is ideal) and fix it with both top and bottom rubbers to fish two maggots on a size 16 hook just on the bottom. A good starting pattern for shot arrangement is to place one BB 10 inches

from the hook, and another directly beneath the float. In mild weather bites should prove to be both positive and regular provided you loose-feed half a dozen or so maggots every other cast — just enough to keep the shoal interested in fact, but remember to stop loose-feeding if bites stop. If this happens you could step down to a smaller hook or try altering tactics and presenting the bait really hard on the bottom by moving the float up a foot or so and fixing it bottom end only.

Alternatively, the roach may want a falling bait. Swap the bottom BB shot for several tiny ones and fix a single one 18 inches from the hook with the rest up under the float, which has been slid back to its original depth and double rubber presentation.

The technique is to measure how long it now takes for the lighter bottom shot to sink the float down to its final position (it quickly cocks at first due to the bulk shot immediately beneath it), and strike if it takes longer than it should. This indicates that a roach has intercepted the bait on the way down, and is holding up the tiny bottom shot. This is a particularly effective way of catching roach occupying the upper water layers. Use light baits such as a single maggot or caster.

These same basic methods work just as effectively at greater distances, particularly in gravel pits if fishing depressions between gravel bars. Plummet carefully, and to ensure the bait stays where you want it, always distance-fish with an antenna-type float fixed bottom end only. Cast well beyond the swim and put your rod tip below the surface before reeling tackle back over the baited swim. This ensures a completely sunken line — the only way of beating wind drift and surface tow. Keep a small bottle of washing-up liquid handy, and sponge this liberally on to the reel spool if new line proves difficult to sink. Loose feed of maggots or casters may be placed in not too-distant swims by catapult, or mixed in with a stiff groundbait and either catapulted or thrown to much further swims. For a good stiff groundbait mix 6 parts breadcrumbs to one part of flaked maize and do not over-soak. The largest of stillwater roach invariably fall to large offerings of breadflake legered over a carpet of light cereal groundbait containing mashed bread. Try a simple fixed paternoster with a $\frac{1}{2}$ oz bomb on a 12 inch link and a size 10 hook on a 16 inch tail. Use two rests with the leger rod pointing directly at the bait, and after tightening up the bomb, clip on an indicator bobbin between reel and butt

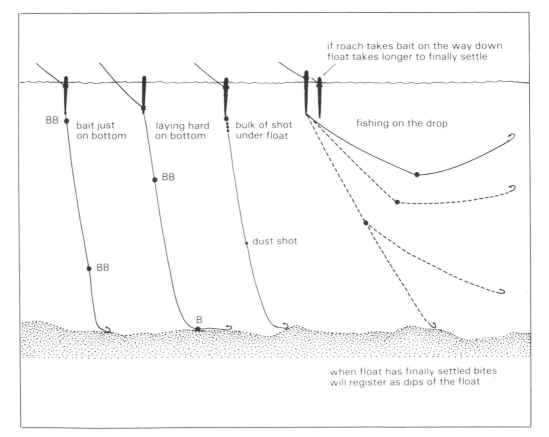

Different rigs for roach fishing in stillwater.

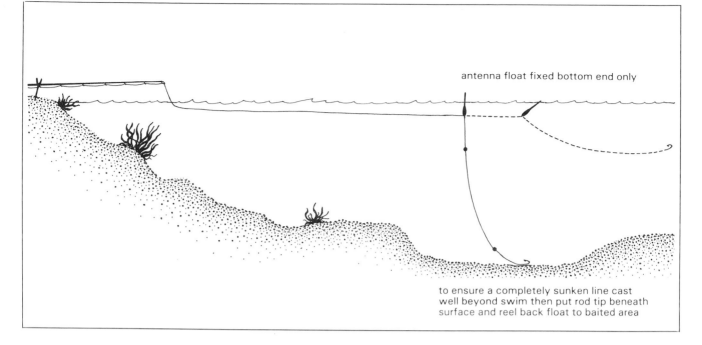

antenna float fixed bottom end only

to ensure a completely sunken line cast
well beyond swim then put rod tip beneath
surface and reel back float to baited area

ring. Allow the bobbin a drop of around 12 inches, and hit any slow or positive movement unless only twitches materialize — in which case change down to smaller hooks and use smaller baits. Best results with larger roach invariably occur in periods of low light such as at dawn, dusk or after dark, after groundbait has first been introduced. Use a luminous Beta light bobbin rather than a torch when fishing at night, because everything from casting to playing and netting fish is far easier if your natural night eyes are allowed to function. It is surprising how much you can see and do after a short time in the dark without a torch, if everything is to hand and you are familiar with the layout and general surroundings of the swim.

Basic tackle techniques and control do not vary all that much in running water, except that 'trotting' a bait through a swim does demand a little more skill than presenting a static bait in still water. You need to keep a controlled line between float and rod tip, but not so tight that the float is over-checked and the bait is pulled unnaturally against the current. Maggots and lumps of bread do not swim upstream, and roach become suspicious of food which rolls along the bottom in a different manner to the unattached fragments all around it; from a very early age they learn to leave well alone. Hence 6 inch roach are usually easy to catch, and it becomes harder from there upwards. So practise the art of trotting with a fixed-spool reel, first

ensuring your line is in good order and not kinked and that the spool is well filled, so that loops roll easily from the rim when you need to give line as the current takes the float downstream from an open bale arm. Use your forefinger to lock the spool in between gentle 'lifts' of the 13 foot rod, so you are in contact whenever the float dips. When this happens turn the reel handle in one movement to put the bale arm over, and remove your forefinger from the spool. You are then, hopefully, connected to a roach. In running water these will usually fight harder, so do not be in a hurry or you will pull the hook out. It is a good way to catch roach, particularly during the winter months when the bottom is clean after the weeds have been scoured out by floods.

Cold water roach have a definite bluish tinge to their normally golden flanks. They often prefer long, steady-paced glides to their deeper summer quarters on the bends, which may have been turned into vast swirling eddies. Indeed the secret in choosing roach swims during the colder months is to opt for steady water instead of swims which boil on the surface and where the bottom currents change direction every few minutes. Roach like a stable environment where food is brought down to them in a leisurely fashion, so try to present the bait just tripping bottom. The way to achieve this is by careful plummeting of the swim and exact float fixing. In calm conditions use rubbers top and bottom so that the float is whisked from the

Fishing the depressions in a gravel pit using an antenna float fixed bottom-end only.

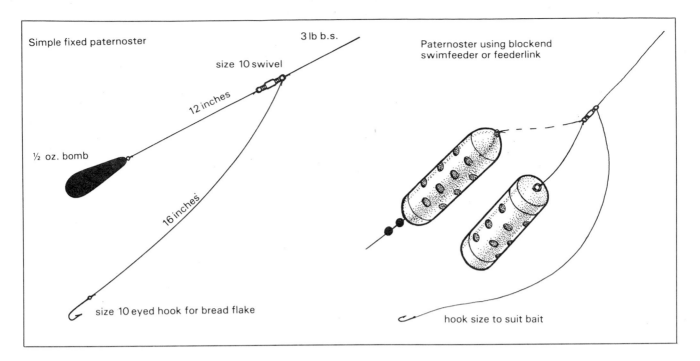

Simple fixed paternoster

3 lb b.s.

size 10 swivel

12 inches

½ oz. bomb

16 inches

size 10 eyed hook for bread flake

Paternoster using blockend swimfeeder or feederlink

hook size to suit bait

Two types of paternoster rig for roach fishing.

A bobbin indicator with a swan shot pinched immediately below.

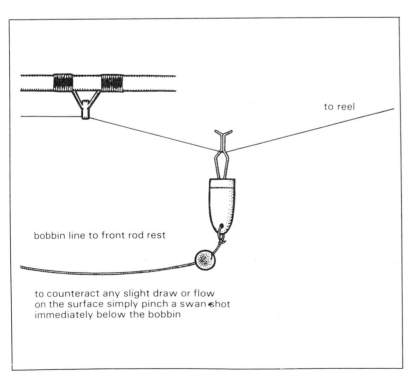

to reel

bobbin line to front rod rest

to counteract any slight draw or flow on the surface simply pinch a swan shot immediately below the bobbin

surface on the strike with the least disturbance. Streamlined stick floats or balsa-bodied sticks and Avon trotters are all ideal.

In windy conditions use a bottom-bodied float like a ducker for stability, and sink the line for a steady run through. In gentle currents put a small shot within 12 inches of the hook and the bulk shot evenly distributed up the line. But in fast water you must get the bait down quickly by fixing at least half the shot within 10 inches of the hook and the rest at mid-depth. Do not be afraid to experiment until you get it right.

In deep, fast rivers legering really comes into its own. Use a blockend swimfeeder or Feederlink to concentrate maggots or casters next to the hookbait and a fixed paternoster rig. Simply exchange the bomb for a swimfeeder and choose a hook size to suit the bait.

For bite indication watch the rod tip, or screw in a quivertip for a much finer registration. If the tip suddenly springs back — as opposed to the tap-tap of a downstream bite — this should still be struck, as a roach may have moved across the current with the bait and dislodged the feeder.

In very slow rivers — particularly when summer weed holds the flow up — all the techniques mentioned for stillwater fishing may be used.

Laying-on with the float set well over depth often accounts for those better quality fish which prefer a static bait on the bottom in the deepest part of the swim. Try a bunch of maggots or a lump of bread-flake, both on a size 10 hook. And when legering the really slow river swims you can even use a leger bobbin for more sensitive bite indication, just the same as for gravel pit legering. To counteract any slight draw or flow on the surface, simply pinch a swan shot immediately below the bobbin. In small rivers or overgrown streams where thick weed makes most techniques impossible, but where roach can easily be seen between the weedy

runs, freelining can be the answer. Use the bare hook, say a size 12, 10 or 8, tied direct to 3 lb breaking strain line. No float, shot or leger bombs. You carefully flip a lump of breadflake or a worm well upstream at the head of the shoal and watch either the bait, or the line where it enters the water as the current carries the bait along the bottom. If you have been stealthy in your approach,

bites will be bold, and more often than not in these small but rich little waters the average size roach will be large. Use Polaroid sunglasses which cut out reflected light, and walk as quietly as possible, picking up your feet at each step. If the roach do not know you are there, at least a couple are yours. Then it is best to move onto another shoal and rest the swim.

John Wilson quiver tipping for river roach using legered breadflake.

Rudd

Rudd are lovers of stillwaters. They are often taken from the same swims as roach, on the same bait, at the same depth, on identical tackle and at the same time of day. Rudd and roach are even occasionally mistaken for each other. But unless you catch a hybrid which shows characteristics of both, it is not difficult to identify rudd by its golden scales, which on average are slightly larger than those of the roach, and its brilliant orange-red fins. It also has much longer lower lips, and it is this protruding bottom jaw which suggests that rudd spend much of their feeding time searching for nymphs and other morsels in the upper water layers.

Rudd are also great shoal fish, like roach, and usually tend to group very much according to size. You may catch rudd after rudd, all of exactly the same size, and then suddenly take a spate of much larger or smaller fish as a new shoal moves into the swim. On those humid-overcast summer evenings when a really black night seems imminent as dusk draws near, the very largest rudd of all may put in an appearance.

Generally, however, and regardless of size, the rudd is a very bold biter — whether you fish fine or heavy, on the bottom or on the surface, it is a far more gullible fish than the roach.

Both the 13 foot float rod and 9-11 foot leger rod recommended for roaching will suit rudd fishing admirably, as will reel and line choice plus all the sundry items.

No fish is more inclined to wander than rudd on a warm summer's day. Where hatches of flies are emerging from their nymph cases in the surface film, rudd are bound to be watching somewhere below. The protruding lower jaw is purpose-built for sucking down such surface morsels. On a windy day the rudd shoals chase food all over the place, and there is no better way to observe their feeding patterns and to get to know the species than on a shallow, weedy lake. If the water is clear and warm, the fish themselves may even be seen darting about. Float fishing is the way to catch rudd. A particularly effective set-up, using a 2-4 inch length of peacock quill or sarkandas reed with a large shot fixed both above and below to facilitate long casting, is illustrated. This 'flat float' set-up is very useful for presenting surface baits such as small pieces of breadcrust or floating casters. For best results the float should be fixed double rubber between two and four feet above the hook, and the line from hook to reel given a light smear with Mucilin line floatant. Then, when a rudd sucks in the bait the float simply slides along the surface. Catapult a small

The 'flat float' for presenting surface baits.

hook 2—4 feet from float

2-4 inch peacock quill or sarkansas reed fixed double rubber with a large shot at either end

to rod

line from hook to reel given smear of line floatant

yet steady stream of loose feed around the float to keep the shoal interested, and be prepared to move stealthily along the bank or even over to the other side of the lake if wind drift takes the shoals on to a different course. This is the most exciting method of taking rudd. If bites on the surface slow up because the rudd start to become suspicious, change the loose feed over from floating to sinking casters or maggots. Degrease the line between hook and float with washing-up liquid or by pulling it slowly through a pinch of bankside mud. But keep the line floating from float to rod for a quick strike.

When rudd cannot be seen and the introduction of floating baits does not encourage a rise, such as in cool summer weather or overcast rainy conditions, try searching right in the middle of weedbeds. Entire shoals sometimes prefer the sanctuary of cover overhead in dim light, or the nearby protection of thick reedbeds. Reedbeds also harbour a lot of natural food. On windless days individual stems can sometimes be seen 'knocking' or twitching as rudd peck off snails, nymphs and other food items. If you own a pair of binoculars, spend a while observing possible haunts before choosing a swim. To get the most from reedbeds, cast the float to settle really close to the stems. A zoomer or loaded antenna is the best type of float for this situation because it flies through the air like a dart ahead of the weights and hook. If the float is not checked too hard during casting you will, after a little practice, be able almost to bounce the float off the leading stems, so the bait glides down to settle directly beneath, just inches from the reeds. Sometimes bites may come 'on the drop' and sometimes you may have to wait several minutes with the bait lying on the bottom before it is picked up. Put any additional shot which the float takes at around mid-depth. If bites only occur on the bottom, and indications on the float are hard to distinguish, move the shot to within six inches of the bait to show a more positive bite. Either way be prepared to

One can expect positive bite indications on the bobbin when using big baits like breadflake, even in winter. Here, John Wilson is about to strike.

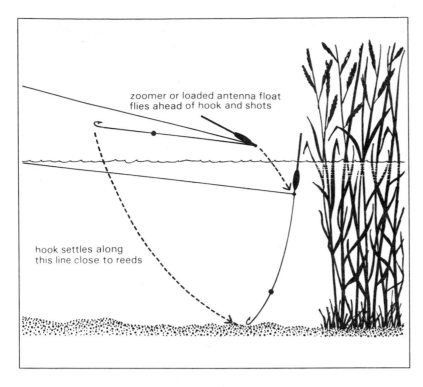

zoomer or loaded antenna float flies ahead of hook and shots

hook settles along this line close to reeds

Presenting baits close to reedbeds using a zoomer or loaded antenna float.

To present breadflake on top of bottom weeds you can use long hook and leger weight links. These can be varied according to the suspected height of the weed.

experiment, and to catapult some hookbait samples into the reeds every so often to keep the shoal interested. Breadflake is a good bait where rudd are hiding between reed stems and want to play the waiting game, and it is usually a good quality fish which finally comes out. Bites will naturally be far fewer if a group of bigger but less numerous fish is contacted so do not be in too much of a hurry to strike. Allow the float to disappear before setting the hook if using larger baits which require bigger hooks to hold them. Any rudd weighing more than a pound will think nothing of swallowing a piece of flake the size of a 2p piece hiding a size 8 hook. Nevertheless when the hook goes home

you must bully the fish at once lest it threads its way into the reeds. So choose a 3 lb breaking strain line and tie hooks direct.

Although it might sound contradictory, many good rudd are caught by legering with either breadflake, worms, maggots or sweetcorn. It just goes to show how obliging this fish is! During the winter, shallow waters which warm up quickly during spells of mild weather are preferred, while in the summer months weedy, well established old gravel pits take a lot of beating for regularly producing rudd. In summer, an hour before dark, deposit a good carpet of cereal groundbait containing mashed bread on the bottom of a medium-depth bar or plateau.

Movement areas sometimes become quite obvious if you visit the same water regularly, because after a warm day rudd invariably roll and wander along the same course during the evenings.

However, when you have no visible evidence to go on, do some careful work with a plummet and select a shelf or a gravel plateau leading up from much deeper water. If there are patches of surface weed close by, so much the better — it will give the rudd shoals more confidence to feed on the shallows. Gaps between tree-covered islands which provide shade during the daytime are always worth attention, as are any definite bays or entrances to dykes in pits.

After the commotion of heaving in the groundbait has subsided, there is usually a long lull in which to tackle up and get settled in. Then, just before darkness falls, rudd may be seen rolling over or near the

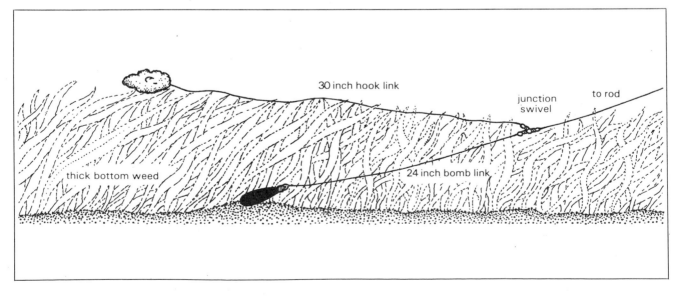

30 inch hook link

junction swivel

to rod

thick bottom weed

24 inch bomb link

A catch of three specimen rudd and a tench.

baited area. Bites can be expected shortly afterwards.

At night, at really short range — say up to 3 rod lengths out — a Beta light luminous float with a rating of at least 400 microlamberts is useful for those who prefer float fishing. And where casting beyond weedbeds into clear channels is necessary, there is no other way. Legering, however, is far less trouble and more productive overall taking all sorts of weather combinations into account.

Set the 9-11 foot leger rod in two rests pointing at the bait ready to receive a Beta light bobbin indicator. Terminal tackle depends very much on bottom weed. If there is little or none, a standard-length pater-

noster as recommended for roach legering is ideal. If, however, you are obliged to present the breadflake hookbait on top of weed, you must use much longer hook and lead links. Hook sizes 10-16 should be tied direct to the 3 lb reel line. In really heavy weed use breadcrust on the hook, which being more buoyant than flake, will not become hidden. There are summer nights when rudd seem willing to feed right through until dawn. But they are rare indeed, and if at around midnight there has not been a bite for quite some time, the next feeding spell may not come until the shoals start moving again at dawn.

In winter, if you select a fairly shallow lake or pit containing a good stock of rudd

Fishing a lake for rudd
using maggots on float
fishing tackle.

and wait for a spell of mild weather (particularly in a south-westerly airstream), then the chance to take a good haul of fish is really on the cards. Rod and tackle rigs remain the same as legering in the summer, except that a step down to smaller hooks ranging from 10 to 16 is recommended to hold either breadflake or maggots respectively.

To concentrate loose feed close to your hookbait use an open-ended swimfeeder plugged each end with a dryish breadcrumb mix, with maggots in the middle if you are using them on the hook. The groundbait really does need to be hardly wet, so that as the feeder lands on the bottom it expands, exploding the contents all around the hookbait.

Casters are also a good winter rudd bait which fit nicely into the feeder, and there

is, of course, nothing to stop you using chopped pieces of worm if a lobtail is put on the hook, or sweetcorn (although this seems to work on only a few waters in the winter).

Even in winter one can expect really positive bite indications on the bobbin when using big baits like breadflake. But with, say, two maggots on size 16 hook, 'twitches' and just inch 'lifts' are very often the only signs of bites. The method then is simply to strike at anything.

In calm or not too windy conditions, float fishing with bait hard on the bottom and using an antenna float with the line well sunk from float to rod is another good way of taking winter rudd. It is a particularly effective way of hitting those tiny bites experienced when legering with small baits.

Tench

Although tench live in many rivers, sometimes growing to quite large proportions, they are first and foremost a species of stillwaters, that is of ponds, pits, lakes and meres. By nature they are a ponderous, deliberate, seemingly docile fish, but when hooked always a powerful dogged fighter. There is a tradition that there is no better quarry with which to start the coarse season. Tench are always most active during the summer months, with peak potential being from mid-June until around the end of August. June and July, however are probably *the* tenching months, because tench go on a feeding spree immediately before and after spawning.

Of all the ways to catch tench, by far and away the most exciting is to float fish close in between patches of lilies or alongside reedbeds.

The rod should be 11 to 12 feet long with a nice easy, all-through action, coupled to a fixed-spool reel holding 4 lb breaking strain line with hooks tied direct. For picking up line and setting the hook at greater distances, particularly when legering far out using swimfeeder rigs etc., a fast taper rod of around 11 feet with a $1\frac{1}{4}$ lb test curve is ideal, with the reel line increased to 6 lb breaking strain.

Tench have a peculiar way of feeding — they stand on their noses to suck in the bait and return to an even keel whilst chewing it. They are equipped with powerful teeth that will split a worm into pulp or crush the juice and innards from maggots, before the fish spits out the hook as an indigestible and undesirable object. This is why an angler whose tackle is incorrectly shotted will reel in time and time again with just empty maggot skins on the hook. The secret is to set up your float overdepth, attached bottom end only, with one or two large shot positioned just 3-4 inches from the hook. This is known as the 'lift method' because when the tench dislodges the shot as it sucks the bait from the bottom,

the float lifts up and may even fall flat. You can strike while the float is falling over because the tench will have the bait well in its mouth.

Sometimes the float will cock again and just glide under as the tench moves off to another patch of bait. But it is best not to wait in case it spits the hook out, so learn to strike quickly as the float starts to lift.

Buoyant floats like peacock quill or sarkandas reed are ideal for 'lift fishing'. They sometimes almost pop out of the water, but more important, a buoyant float (as opposed to a loaded one) actually supports the weight of the shots as the tench sucks the bait up. Remember that when the float is lying flat the tench is supporting the weights.

Always gear hook size to bait size: a whole lobworm on a size 6; a good lump of breadflake on a size 8 or 10; maggots, casters or sweetcorn on sizes 10 to 14 depending on whether you try single or

John Wilson unhooking an early season tench caught from a shallow lake using a swimfeeder rig baited with maggots. See page 48 for the same fish being netted.

Above John Wilson landing a tench.

Opposite Andy Barker with a fine gravel pit tench weighing 7 lb 15 oz.

bunch baits. In recent years the effectiveness of sweetcorn as a tench bait has been proven just about everywhere. Each water needs to be treated and fished differently. The tench in a carp lake, for instance, may show a distinct preference for high-protein baits such as trout pellet paste, sausage meat, and so on, because the water has been heavily pre-baited by carp enthusiasts. There are, in fact, very few baits which tench will not pick up at one time or another, but the angler will initially catch more tench by keeping to the simple ones.

When searching a new water for good tench swims, try to arrive as dawn breaks to catch the early morning bubblers. Walk slowly and stealthily around for a while and you will notice very definite feeding areas where patches of tiny needle bubbles made by tench can be seen in the same spots morning after morning. These are natural swims where tench root about along the bottom, feeding confidently on bloodworms and other bottom-dwelling delicacies. Sometimes the bubbling continues until the sun is well up. Then the tench stop moving until the evening, when bubbling may resume. In other swims the bubbling activity may last for just an hour or so before the tench vacate the area and move on to follow a definite feeding route, spending the brightest part of the day in the sanctuary of either very deep or very

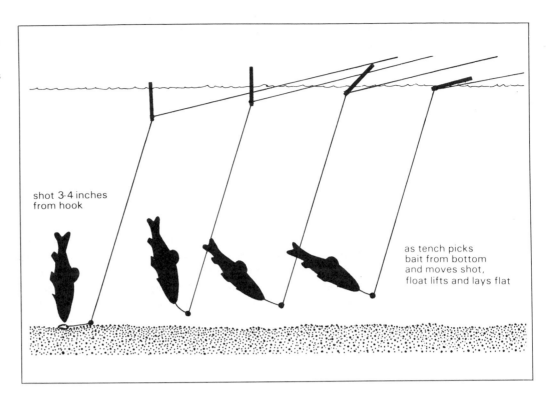

The 'lift' method of tench fishing. As the tench picks the bait up from the bottom and moves the shot, the float lifts and lays flat on the surface.

shot 3-4 inches from hook

as tench picks bait from bottom and moves shot, float lifts and lays flat

weedy water. Find these areas and you will be able to catch tench at any time of the day.

A problem that sometimes occurs with bubbling tench, even when there appear to be plenty of them rooting about on the bottom and the surface looks like a witches' cauldron, is that you cannot get them to take your hookbait. The frustration is unbelievable. Scaling down to light lines and small hooks, say a size 16 holding just a single maggot, might produce the odd

bite, but it is unnerving fishing ultra light, especially anywhere near weedbeds where a lost fish may be the result. So it is better to attack the problem with a larger bait like a big lobworm.

When float fishing the tench may become suspicious of a vertical line, so on these occasions switch over to freelining the lob on a size 6 hook. No shots, float or leger. The worm is cast out well beyond the bubbles and allowed to free-fall down to the bottom. The rod is then set in two rests pointing at the bait, with the line hanging down in a definite bow from rod tip to surface. First allow any tench on the outskirts of the main group the chance of picking up the lob, before slowly twitching it back along the bottom, six inches at a time. Watch the line carefully, because bites will be sudden and often quite savage. Change direction with each successive cast, and beware of those drop-back bites when the line suddenly falls slack as a tench sucks in the bait and swims towards you.

Thick weed, because of the cover and food it contains, has always been favourable for tench fishing, and to get the best from really weedy waters you must be prepared to rake out a swim. A couple of garden rake heads lashed together, wrapped with lead pipe for added weight, plus several yards of stout nylon rope will suffice. The plan is to take out sufficient weed

Freelining worms or other large baits.

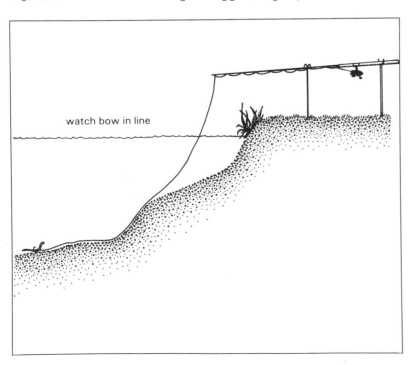

watch bow in line

to enable the swim to be fished, and to cloud the bottom up with all the usual goodies upon which tench generally feed. Fishing is often worthwhile immediately after raking, while everything is in suspension. Do not let the commotion put you off, because the tench may even be attracted by it. Alternatively, you could try raking in the evening and adding some groundbait containing samples of the hookbait you will be using the following morning. Worms seem to work especially well after raking, with chopped worms as feed and using brandlings on the hook.

In larger waters including clear, shallow lakes where the tench always seem to keep well out because the marginal water is so shallow, or there is a lack of weed, distance legering with a swimfeeder rig is the answer.

Do not worry about the heavy splash of a feeder regularly hitting the surface, for even in very shallow water tench quickly learn to associate its arrival with another helping of free food. You create your own tench swim, in fact, with fish eagerly moving about on the bottom from one pile of bait to another. So casting needs to be accurate, or you will spread both bait and tench all over the place. It is often a good bet to use two rods with identical rigs, and to cast quite frequently for at least an hour, even if bites do not materialize, just to bait up the area. The fast-taper rods are set low to the water to minimize line drag, and point directly at the bait. Remember that in shallow water a low sideways strike will pick up maximum line on the strike, whereas in deep water an upward sweep is required.

As for feeder rigs, a simple paternoster set up is ideal, and although reel line needs to be 6 lb breaking strain for a loaded feeder, the actual hook link can be lighter if small baits are being used on small hooks. If you use, say, a 3 lb or 4 lb hook link holding a size 14 and two maggots, remember when a good tench nears the net that you are actually on much lighter tackle than the 6 lb reel line. Fine hooklengths have little chance of breaking when striking or whilst playing tench at distance. It is only when the fish comes close in that you need to be careful.

Open-ended feeders are best for still-water work, and you need to mix the groundbait just right for plugging the free bait in at both ends. Coarse breadcrumbs,

only just dampened, are ideal because they really explode the contents out as the feeder hits bottom. Sweetcorn, casters and maggots all work well both as hookbaits and feeder filling, as do cocktails and mixtures of each. Over fine weed, the buoyant qualities of two floating casters on the hook can prove effective. To stop feeder maggots from burrowing into blanket weed or silt, immerse them for five seconds only in boiling water and dry off with breadcrumbs.

Just plain breadflake is of course an excellent hookbait when pumping out a lot of crumbs. At this point do not wind the feeder along the bottom, separating hookbait from feed. Tighten up gently to sink line fully in a straight line before clipping on a bobbin indicator. If there is a strong wind try to fish directly into it, or pinch a swan shot or two on to the bobbin line to stop an underwater bow forming between

Two methods of striking in shallow and deep still-waters.

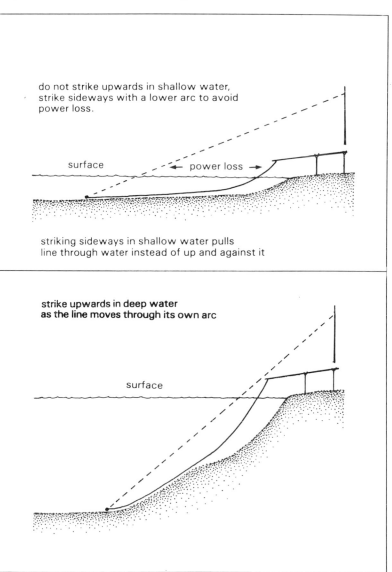

do not strike upwards in shallow water, strike sideways with a lower arc to avoid power loss.

surface ← power loss →

striking sideways in shallow water pulls line through water instead of up and against it

strike upwards in deep water as the line moves through its own arc

surface

John Wilson playing a
tench taken on leger
tackle.

feeder and rod tip in crosswinds. If the line
is not reasonably tight between feeder and
rod, setting the hook becomes more of a
problem the further out you fish.

During the first few sessions of feeder
fishing a new swim, bites will invariably
show as a really positive lift of the bobbin
as the tench quickly moves from one patch
of bait to another, so set it on a drop of
around 18 inches. As the tench become
more preoccupied on the loose feed however, and as your casting becomes more
accurate, concentrating fish within a much
smaller area, quite a lot of tiny 'twitch' bites
will result. The bobbin (set now on a much
shorter drop) will merely lift or drop back
an inch or so at a time. This hardly looks
like tench bites. But if you reel in sucked
maggot skins, you have in fact missed a
very confident bite. The hook must have
been sucked back to the throat teeth,
chewed for a while and then spat out. So
hit any slight twitch, jingle or shake of the
bobbin once the twitching cycle has be-
gun. On calm days forget the bobbin and
simply watch the line where it enters the
water.

During those long all-day sessions
where concentration on the line or bobbins becomes difficult to maintain, electronic bite alarms or indicators used as the
front rod rest ahead of the bobbin are a
really worthwhile addition. For daytime
fishing both fluorescent yellow and red
coloured bobbins catch the eye very well,
and for fishing at night, luminous Beta
light bobbins are an enormous advantage.
In very clear waters where daytime sessions fail to produce any consistent
catches of tench, night fishing could be
the answer. Such waters are quite rare, but
they do exist.

Glossary

Arlesey bomb a pear-shaped leger lead incorporating a swivel – designed for tangle-free long-distance casting.

A.C.A. abbreviation for the Anglers' Cooperative Association, an organisation that fights pollution on behalf of anglers.

Bait any edible substance used to tempt fish to take the hook.

Backwater offshoot of main river with little or no flow.

Bale-arm wire arm that picks up the line and guides it onto the spool of a fixed-spool reel.

Balsa lightweight wood from which float bodies are often made. Also the name given to a type of float that is fished top-and-bottom and is used in fast, streamy water.

Bank stick metal pole incorporating a $\frac{3}{8}$" BSF thread for the attachment of a rod rest or a keepnet.

Barb small projection near the point of a hook to ensure a secure hold.

Barbules small, fleshy feelers (probably taste organs) found on the mouths of barbel, tench, carp and gudgeon.

Bar spoon artificial lure comprising a spoon blade that is attached to a bar by means of a saddle-shackle.

Bite the result of the bait being taken by a fish. (*See* run.)

Bivouac a special type of umbrella-tent used by night fishermen.

Blank sections of tubular glass or carbon fibre from which a rod is made.
Also the term applied by anglers to a fishless session.

Block-end feeder a swim-feeder with sealed ends.

Bloodworms tiny red worms found in the mud at the bottom of stagnant water. They are frequently used in conjunction with Continental styles of pole fishing. (See 'Pole'.)

Bobbin a bite indicator that is attached to the line and hung between the reel and the butt ring, or between the butt ring and second ring. A small piece of dough was once commonly used for the purpose but nowadays a plastic bottle-top is more popular.

Brandling a small yellow-ringed worm found in manure heaps.

Breaking strain the amount of pull that line will withstand before it breaks.

Bread punch a small tube which punches out tiny pellets of bread for bait.

B.R.F.C. abbreviation for British Record Fish Committee.

Butt the handle section of a fishing rod.

Buzzer electric or electronic battery operated bite alarm used mainly by carp anglers.

Cast the act of propelling the terminal tackle to the required spot.

Casters maggot chrysalids in an early stage of development at which stage they sink.

Caudal fin Tail fin.

Check the audible ratchet on a reel.

Close-season the period from March 15th to June 15th inclusive when coarse fishing is not permitted (local variations may occur).

Clutch adjustable tension by means of which line can be yielded from a fixed-spool reel.

Dead bait dead fish used as bait for pike, zander and eels.

Disgorger a tool for the removal of hooks that have been taken deep.

Dorsal fin back fin.

Double rubber see top and bottom.

Draw selection of pegs in an angling competition. (*See* peg.)

Drain Man-made waterway for the purpose of draining low-lying land.

Eddy a spot that is sheltered from the main flow of a river where the current has a circular motion.

Feed edible items introduced into the water to induce fish to remain in the area and seek out the hook-bait.

Ferrule the means by which the sections of a rod may be joined together. (*See* spigot.)

Float buoyant aid to bite indication and bait presentation. (*See* balsa, peacock, quill, sarkandas, stick float and waggler.)

Float-leger a form of legering whereby bite indication is provided by a float.

Flow the current in a river, or the water movement created by wind in a lake or pit.

Free-line a method of fishing in which no float or lead is used on the line.

Fry young fish shortly after hatching.

Gaff a large hook on a shaft that was once commonly used for landing pike but is now rarely used by coarse fishermen.

Gentles another name for maggots.

Gozzer a home-bred white maggot with a translucent skin — it is rated by many anglers as the very best bait for bream.

Groundbait any sort of cereal that is dampened and compressed into a ball to carry feed items or create a cloud. Proprietary groundbait is available but most anglers use pure breadcrumb.

Holdall a container for transporting rods, landing net, rod rests and umbrella.

Hook-link the length of line to which the hook is attached. (Sometimes referred to as a hook-length.)

H.P. or H.N.V. baits High Protein or High Nutritive Value baits used mainly by carp specialists.

Isotope plastic encased luminous glass phial incorporated in bobbin indicators for night fishing.

Jack a small pike.

Keep net a cylindrical net for the live retention of fish.

Landing net a net used to lift a hooked fish from the water so as not to put undue strain on the rod tip or line.

Lead a weight used for legering or paternostering. Many designs are available, the most useful being the Arlesey bomb, the pear lead and the drilled bullet.

Leger a method of presenting a bait on or near the bottom using a weighted terminal tackle.

Line bite a false bite indication produced by a fish swimming into the line.

Line grease proprietary preparation for ensuring that line floats.

Link a length of nylon line to which a leger or paternoster lead is attached.

Link leger a method of legering whereby the weight is fastened to a sliding nylon link.

Live bait live fish used as bait for pike, perch, zander and occasionally chub and barbel.

Lob/lobworm a large lawn worm that may be collected by torchlight on damp, windless nights.

Lure imitation fish which flash, spin or wriggle on being retrieved through the water. They are used to catch pike, zander, perch and chub. (*See* plug and spinner.)

Maggots larval form of fly, used as both hook-bait and feed. They may be used natural white or dyed — the most popular dye colours being bronze, anatto (yellow) and chrysodine (orange). (*See* gozzer, pinkie and squatt.)

Margin the edge of a lake, river or canal.

Match an angling competition.

Mono abbreviation for monofilament — single filament nylon or perlon line.

N.A.C. abbreviation for National Anglers' Council, an advisory body for the sport of angling.

N.F.A. abbreviation for the National Federation of Anglers, an administrative body for coarse anglers in general and match anglers in particular.

Particle baits small seed baits such as sweetcorn, wheat, maple peas, haricot beans, tares and hempseed.

Paste a bait made by mixing stale breadcrumbs or flour with water until the consistency of dough is achieved. Flavoured pastes made with pet-food, cheese and luncheon meat are also popular.

Paternoster a form of leger tackle in which the hook-link is tied at right angles to the main line.

Peacock a popular float making material obtained from the long tail feathers of a peacock.

Pectoral fins the pair of fins adjacent to the gill covers.

Peg a numbered fishing position in a match.

Peg-leg colloquial term applied to the method of float attachment whereby the float is secured bottom-end only.

Pelvic fins the pair of fins situated on the underbelly.

Pick-up *see* bale-arm.

Pinkie a very small pale pink maggot used mainly as a feeder.

Pitch an area of a stillwater adjacent to an angler's fishing position. (*See* swim.)

Plug an artificial lure designed to dive and wriggle when retrieved. It is most commonly used to catch pike but in smaller sizes it can be effective for zander, perch and chub. Also a plug of groundbait used to prevent feed items spilling from an open-ended swim-feeder as it is being cast.

Plummet a detachable lead weight used to measure the depth.

Pole an ultra-light ringless fishing rod made from hollow glass or carbon fibre.

Quill float body material from a bird's feather or a porcupine spine.

Quivertip a very solid glass rod top extension for the detection of bites when legering.

Redworm small, red coloured worm found in compost and well rotted manure heaps.

Rest a means of supporting the rod. At its simplest it can be a stick with a 'vee' shaped top, but most anglers use a bank-stick onto which a specially designed head is attached.

Rings line guides on a fishing rod.

Run a bite that takes line from the open spool of a reel.

Sarkandas a special reed that is used to make floats, notably wagglers. It was originally used as a substitute for peacock but is now popular in its own right.

Skimmer a colloquial term for a small bream.

Slider a special float that slides on the line. It is used when fishing deeper water than can comfortably or efficiently be fished with a fixed float.

Snag an obstruction on which tackle or a hooked fish may be lost.

Snap tackle a hook rig used for pike fishing comprising a pair of treble hooks on a wire trace.

Spade-end a type of hook that has a flattened shank-end to prevent the knot slipping off.

Spate when a river is high and coloured due to rain.

Specimen an exceptionally large fish. Anglers who specialise in the capture of outsize fish are known as specimen hunters.

Spigot a glass rod ferrule.

Split ring a small metal ring used for joining nylon or wire — it is also used to secure the hook and swivel to some types of spinner.

Split shot small spherical lead weights slit to enable them to be pinched on the line.

Squatt a small feeder maggot that due to its rather sluggish nature can be incorporated into a ball of groundbait without causing it to break up.

Stick float a special float made from balsa and cane for smooth flowing shallow to medium depth water. It is unsuitable for deep or turbulent water.

Stop knot a sliding knot used to set the depth when a sliding float is used.

Strike a sharp movement to set the hook.

Swivel a small metal device comprising two eyes that turn independently. It is used as a means of joining lengths of line or wire and as a junction between the two. It is also used when spinning to prevent line twist.

Swim a section of river being fished. (*See* pitch.)

Swim-feeder a cylindrical plastic container that is attached to the line and filled with feed items which spill or crawl out after casting. It is used in conjunction with leger or paternoster tackle. (*See* block-end feeder.)

Swing tip a swinging arm bite indicator that is attached to the rod top by means of a flexible nylon or silicon rubber hinge. It is used when legering in still or very slow moving water.

Tail the distance between hook and lead when legering.

Test Curve the means by which the power of a rod is indicated — being the pull required to position the tip at right angles to the butt.

Top and bottom the method of float attachment whereby a float is secured at both its top and bottom end. This is sometimes termed 'double-rubber'.

Trace a special hook-link made from wire. It is used for pike and less commonly for zander and eels to prevent them biting through the line.

Treble a three pointed hook used with live or dead fish baits for pike and zander.

Tip the top section of a rod.

Trolling a method of fishing for pike whereby a live bait, dead bait or lure is trailed behind a slowly moving boat. The method is rarely used in U.K. but is popular in Ireland.

Trotting a method of float fishing in a river whereby the tackle is allowed to travel in a controlled manner with the current.

Twitch a delicate bite resulting in a small movement of a bite indicator.

Ventral fin the rear, underside fin — sometimes called the anal fin.

Waggler a float made from peacock or sarkandas, sometimes with a balsa body at its base. It is attached bottom-end only and allowed to run through the swim at the speed of the current.

Weed drag a tool used to remove weed from a pitch. It is usually made from a pair of rake-heads secured back-to-back and tied to a length of strong nylon cord.

Winch fitting the fitting used to secure the reel to the rod handle.

Index

Figures in **bold** refer to main entries; figures in *italic* refer to illustrations.

Measurements given in this book are in imperial, but the
metric units can be found by noting the imperial measurements and
using the following conversion table:

Length	Mass
1 inch = 2.54 centimetres	1 ounce = 28.3 grams
1 foot = 30.48 centimetres	1 pound = 0.45 kilograms
1 yard = 91.44 centimetres	

Acknowledgements

Colour

Angler's Mail 83, R. Felton 87, 103; **Angling Photo Service** W. Howes
title page, 23, 38, 39, 42–43, 50, 51, 75, 91; **A. Barker** 58–59, 90, 115;
J. Bailey 62, 78; **J. Gibbinson** 27; **Hamlyn Publishing Group** John Howard
front jacket insert, 19; **G. Marsden** 10–11, 67, back jacket; **M. Millman**
front jacket, 47; **M. Peters** 14, 15, 79; **R. Westwood** 63, 95; **J. Wilson**
jacket insert, 111, 114.

Black and white

Angler's Mail Felton 86, Keal 35, Nash 84; **Angling Photo Service** W. Howes
8–9, 26, 56; A. Barker 92, 94; **J. Gibbinson** 71, 72–73; **G. Marsden** 68;
M. Millman 12, 25, 28, 52–53, 89; **R. Westwood** 61, 65, 76, 77, 80, 96,
97; **J. Wilson** 48, 96 (bottom), 101, 107, 109, 112, 113, 118.

Line-drawings by Ray Burrows and Tony Wheildon (pages 17, 18, 20, 21, 29, 46)

The publishers would like to thank **Gerry's of Wimbledon** for
the use of their premises and tackle for the photograph on page 19 and the front jacket insert.